STUDY GUIDE
to Accompany

Experiencing the World's Religions

Third Edition

Michael Molloy

Richard Curran Trussell
Pikes Peak Community College
Regis University

Boston   Burr Ridge, IL   Dubuque, IA   Madison, WI   New York
San Francisco   St. Louis   Bangkok   Bogotá   Caracas   Kuala Lumpur
Lisbon   London   Madrid   Mexico City   Milan   Montreal   New Delhi
Santiago   Seoul   Singapore   Sydney   Taipei   Toronto

The *McGraw·Hill* Companies

Mc Graw Hill **Higher Education**

1 2 3 4 5 6 7 8 9 0 DOC/DOC 0 9 8 7 6 5 4

ISBN: 0-07-283509-5

www.mhhe.com

CONTENTS

PREFACE

This guide is designed to enhance your learning experience with Michael Molloy's text, *Experiencing the World's Religions*, Third Edition. The format is fairly straightforward. Learning objectives and chapter summaries carefully follow the text. Fill-in-the-blank test questions are selected primarily from the Key Terms lists and the glossary at the end of the book. The multiple-choice questions further check your knowledge about ideas and concepts. Answers for both appear at the end of each chapter. Short-answer study questions, by chapter section form the largest part of this guide. Space is provided for you to write in your responses. If you can answer these, you have essentially mastered the textbook material. A fun way to utilize the questions and enhance learning is in study circles where students quiz one another.

Many students have difficulty choosing topics for papers. The possible paper topics in this guide will stimulate your thinking. Following these are interreligious comparisons, which could also serve as term paper topics. Even if you don't write a paper that compares and contrasts features of two different religions, it is good to think about these questions. Most of your time will be spent exploring particular religions and mastering their beliefs and practices. But it is certainly worthwhile to occasionally step back and consider the similarities and differences between the variety of religions practiced in the world today.

Each chapter of this guide concludes with reflection exercises. These won't provide further facts and details about religion, but they might engage your imagination and take you to a place where religion touches both the world and the heart. Welcome to the adventure.

Finally, your text includes many photographs and images depicting the artistic expression of religious faith. To find even more such images, visit some of the Web sites listed in the appendix, Internet Resources for World Art.

I'd like to dedicate this study guide to the one who has accompanied me through much of my spiritual journey as a friend, companion, and nudger—my wife, Nancy.

RICHARD CURRAN TRUSSELL

CHAPTER 1

UNDERSTANDING RELIGION

LEARNING OBJECTIVES

After reading this chapter, you should be able to

♦ discuss the role and function of religion in human life.

♦ describe theories of the origin of religion.

♦ describe the series of characteristics used to identify a religion.

♦ discuss conceptions of the sacred.

♦ discuss the importance of symbolism in religion.

♦ explain the three patterns for comparing and contrasting religions.

♦ know the value and benefits of studying religion.

CHAPTER SUMMARY

Religion is one of the most significant efforts to answer the most profound questions of human existence. Where do we come from? What should we do while we are here? Why is there so much suffering and pain in life? What is our ultimate destiny and how do we get there? Religion serves many human needs by helping cope with tragedy, by giving hope for practical benefits or blessings, and by drawing us into a community through which we can accomplish things we could not do on our own. Religion has inspired much of the greatest art in history and reflects our sense of wonder about ourselves and the universe.

Some scholars have speculated about the origins of religion. Some of these theories state that religion grew out of a prescientific attempt to manipulate nature for human ends, or that it was an attempt to appease ancestor spirits, or was simply a projection of childhood fantasies and fears that make us feel more secure in an unfeeling universe. Others have seen religion in a more favorable light, noting that it has a positive influence on people, leads to an integrated relationship with others and the cosmos, that it represents a true encounter with the deepest and most mysterious levels of reality, or that it both reflects and prompts the highest levels of human growth and personal integration.

Scholars today strive to study religion in a way that is unbiased and that assumes all religions are worthy of study. This is difficult since we tend to bring assumptions from the religion in which we were raised or from the dominant culture. Because of the diversity among religions, scholars now talk about elements that appear in varying degrees in the different spiritual paths. They include a belief system, a community that embraces it, central stories called myths, ceremonies or rituals, material expressions, ethical guidelines, characteristic emotions or experiences that occur, and a sense of the sacred. Conceptions of the sacred are very diverse. Examples are a transcendent personal God, an immanent pantheistic power, and polytheism, or multiple gods. Other paths embrace atheism or agnosticism or nontheism.

Use of symbolic images and actions convey religious truth or ideas in a powerful way and may suggest a sort of universal language spoken by religions. The comparative study of religion also has proposed three patterns of similarity and difference among religions. The first pattern concerns beliefs and practices in orientation toward the sacred. It identifies the sacramental, the prophetic, and the mystical orientation. The second pattern deals with views of the world and life, such as the nature of the sacred itself, the nature of the universe and humanity's place in it, conceptions of time, human purpose, the role of words and scriptures, and notions of inclusiveness and exclusiveness. The third pattern addresses views of male and female according to both prescribed social roles and conceptions of deity. These three patterns provide useful reference points for comparison and contrast between religions.

Comparative religions as a discipline has grown in complexity and sophistication in over two hundred years of development. It draws on many disciplines because religion has influenced so many areas of life. Today the study of religion offers many insights and pleasures. It assists us in understanding the experiences of others and helps us to better interpret the complexity of the world and our place in it.

FILL IN THE BLANK

1. Literally meaning "not God," _____ holds that there is no God or gods.

2. The belief in one God is called _____.

3. _____ is the position that God may or may not exist, but the existence of God really cannot be proven.

4. The belief that everything in the universe is divine is called _____.

5. The belief in many gods is called _____.

6. A power existing and operating within nature is said to be _____.

7. A power beyond or not limited by the physical world is said to be _____.

8. Other than the ordinary, the _____ is sometimes expressed or experienced in certain objects, actions, or places.

9. A synonym for a belief system, a _____ implies several beliefs fitting together into a fairly complete and systematic interpretation of the universe and humanity's place in it.

10. A _____ is something fairly concrete and ordinary that can represent and help human beings intensely experience something of greater complexity.

MULTIPLE CHOICE

1. The word *religion* is usually interpreted by scholars to mean
   a. renewal.
   b. worship.
   c. reconnecting.
   d. belief in a higher power.

2. Beliefs enacted and made real through ceremonies, certain objects, or specialized locations or buildings define the characteristic of
   a. ritual.
   b. sacredness.
   c. ethics.
   d. community.

3. Familiar term for the sacred reality, particularly in the Western world.
   a. monotheism
   b. polytheism
   c. transcendent
   d. God

4. Many scholars think that religious symbols
   a. point to some structure that underlies all religions.
   b. account for the origin of religion.
   c. have a literal meaning only.
   d. are a projection of the fear and insecurity of childhood.

5. A state of original purity, a battle to fight disorder, a sacrificial death are examples of
   a. the sacred.
   b. ritual.
   c. projected beliefs.
   d. symbolic stories of transformation.

6. One of the three orientations of religions, focusing on rituals and ceremonies as the path to salvation.
   a. sacramental
   b. prophetic
   c. mystical
   d. communal

7. The orientation that seeks union with a reality greater than oneself.
   a. sacramental
   b. prophetic
   c. mystical
   d. communal

8. The orientation that stresses contact with the sacred by proper belief and by adherence to moral rules.
   a. sacramental
   b. prophetic
   c. mystical
   d. communal

9. Religions that emphasize a creation and a history that is limited and unrepeatable conceive time as
   a. cyclical.
   b. central.
   c. linear.
   d. peripheral.

10. Religions that believe the universe simply moves through endless changes that often repeat themselves conceive time as
   a. cyclical.
   b. central.
   c. linear.
   d. sacred.

11. Religions that are inclusive frequently
   a. emphasize the sacred as distinct from the world and believe that order must be imposed through separation.
   b. gather believers together for elaborate rites and ceremonies.
   c. admit many types of beliefs and practices and stress social harmony.
   d. worship a sole male deity.

12. The female divine is sometimes symbolized by
   a. daggers and trees.
   b. eggs and spirals.
   c. long hair and stars.
   d. rocks and clouds.

13. This common approach to religion stresses following reason rather than religious authority and tries to fit answers into a systematic whole.
   a. mythology
   b. psychology
   c. archeology
   d. philosophy

SHORT-ANSWER STUDY QUESTIONS, BY CHAPTER SECTIONS

Why Is There Religion?

What are some of the questions religion seeks to answer? (pp. 2–3)

Speculations on the Sources of Religion

1. List some of the human needs served by religion. (p. 3)

2. Discuss a theory on origins of religion by one of the thinkers in the reading (Tylor, Frazer, Freud, James, Otto, or Jung) that makes most sense to you at the present time. (pp. 3–5)

3. Why are scholars today hesitant to speak of an evolution of religion from one form to another? (p. 5)

Key Characteristics of Religion

1. What is the problem with the traditional dictionary definition of religion? (p. 5)

2. List the eight elements manifested in varying degrees in religions. (pp. 6–7)

The Sacred

1. Define what is meant by the sacred in religion. (pp. 7–8)

2. Offer some examples of how the sacred is variously understood. (p. 8)

3. How can atheism or agnosticism be considered a religion? (p. 8)

Religious Symbolism

1. Offer some examples of religious symbols and discuss their meaning. (pp. 8–10)

2. How are symbols important in dreams? (p. 9)

Patterns among Religions

Discuss the goal of studying religions in the comparative and historical sense. (p. 11)

First Pattern: Focus of Beliefs and Practices

1. Describe features of the sacramental orientation in conceiving and locating the sacred. (p. 11)

2. Describe the features of the prophetic orientation. (p. 11)

3. Describe the features of the mystical orientation. (pp. 11–12)

4. Discuss ways that the three orientations might be found in the same religious tradition. (p. 12)

Second Pattern: Religious Views of the World and Life

1. What are the eight great questions religions must answer? (p. 12)

2. Review ways that the nature of sacred reality may be conceived. (p. 12)

3. Describe different conceptions of the nature of the universe. (pp. 12–13)

4. Describe the spectrum of attitudes toward nature found in religions. (p. 13)

5. Define linear and cyclical time and the concerns that accompany each. (pp. 13–14)

6. Offer views of human purpose seen in different religions. (p. 14)

7. What place do words and scriptures occupy in religion? (p. 14)

8. How are concepts of inclusiveness and exclusiveness expressed in religion? (p. 14)

Third Pattern: Religious Views of Male and Female

1. What role did female deity play in many cultures and religions? (pp. 15–16)

2. Give some examples of places where Goddess worship is alive today. (Box: p. 15)

3. Offer examples of patriarchal religion overcoming matriarchal elements. (p. 16)

4. What factors point to a change in the status of women in religion? (p. 16)

Multidisciplinary Approaches to the Study of Religion

Discuss the approaches of at least three disciplines to religion (psychology, mythology, philosophy, theology, the arts, anthropology, archeology, comparative religion). (pp. 17–18)

Key Critical Questions

1. Describe the shifting approaches and concerns in the evolution of comparative religions scholarship. (pp. 18–22)

2. What moral questions have emerged in the study of religions? (p. 21)

3. Offer examples of the great diversity manifesting within major world religions. (pp. 21–22)

Why Study the Major Religions of the World?

The author offers ten examples of the pleasures and rewards of the study of religions. Which ones appeal to you now and why? (pp. 22–24)

The Pilgrimage

What might be some of the consequences of undertaking an intellectual pilgrimage to many of the world's important living religions? (p. 24)

Religion beyond the Classroom

1. What are some of the benefits in going beyond just studying books to learn about religion? (pp. 25–26)

2. Which of the options presented by the author appeal to you? (pp. 25–26)

POSSIBLE PAPER TOPICS

1. Your instructor may want you to focus on a particular religion or religions covered in the course rather than write on the more theoretical material presented in this chapter. One of the points made in this chapter was that religions are not permanent theoretical constructs but are constantly in a process of change. You may want to write about certain changes that occurred in one of the religions that will be studied.

2. Research religious symbolism and its meaning.

3. Explore Goddess worship in either ancient or modern times.

INTERRELIGIOUS COMPARISONS

Review the three patterns among religions that scholars use to study religions in a comparative and historical sense. Choose one of the patterns and then look for similarities and differences in two of the religions to be studied in the text. You may even want to limit your research to a particular time period.

REFLECTION EXERCISES

1. The chapter begins with an imagined encounter in the mountains near a friend's cabin that prompts asking big questions about life and the universe. Go back and review them. What has prompted these questions in your life or in the lives of your friends and family? Both positive and negative experiences can evoke such pondering and reflection.

2. Symbols found in religions often have a universal quality. Try taking a basic symbol such as fire or water or one of your choice. Put the word in the center of a page of paper. With radiating spokes coming from it, write down what the object can be used for or how it manifests in the world. As you study the religions in the text, look for your basic symbol to appear, and watch for its characteristics to convey ideas and concepts found in that religion.

3. Consider the eight great questions to which religions must provide answers. How do you currently answer them? At the end of the course, you may want to revisit them and see if your answers have changed. These are also great questions with which to interview others. This could develop into an interesting project. You could interview a cross-section of people or you could explore the diversity within a single tradition.

4. The second pattern of comparison in religions includes views of the world and nature. Reflect on your own views of nature. Have they changed over time? Where on the spectrum of attitudes is your understanding? Interview some friends for their views.

ANSWERS

Fill In the Blank

1. atheism
2. monotheism
3. Agnosticism
4. pantheism
5. polytheism
6. immanent
7. transcendent
8. sacred
9. worldview
10. symbol

Multiple Choice

1. c
2. a
3. d
4. a
5. d
6. a
7. c
8. b
9. c
10. a
11. c
12. b
13. d

CHAPTER 2

ORAL RELIGIONS

LEARNING OBJECTIVES

After reading this chapter, you should be able to

♦ describe the three patterns shared by oral religions.

♦ explain the view of reality held by oral religions.

♦ describe the importance of ritual in the practice of oral religion.

♦ discuss rite-of-passage ceremonies.

♦ define the function of taboos.

♦ describe the role of the shaman.

CHAPTER SUMMARY

Oral religions are practiced by native peoples around the world. Their teachings have been conveyed primarily by word of mouth rather than through written texts. Though a tremendous variety exists in stories, beliefs, and practices among oral religions, certain key patterns emerge.

Oral religions express strong relationships with nature. Human beings are embedded in a world of animals, plants, and a landscape where the life force, or the "spirits," are present in everything. The universe has a visible ordinary reality and a deeper, unseen sacred presence, yet all is part of the same reality with no clear boundaries between the natural and the supernatural. To avoid harm and incur blessings, human beings must treat all things with care. An ethic of restraint or conservation is shown in taking only what one needs and in using all the parts of an animal or a plant. Animals are often spoken of in terms of kinship, as brothers and sisters, or as another tribe or people.

The second pattern among oral religions is a concept of sacred time and space that supports a sense of identity. Participants enter into the sacred time in which live the ancestors and gods through ritually retelling their stories and deeds. By structuring daily life around the mythic events in sacred time, they create a sense of holiness in everyday life. The cyclical nature of sacred time is also seen in following the rhythm of the seasons to observe certain facets of life, such as planting, hunting, or relocating to another area. Sacred space is tied to significant features of the land where tribal peoples live, or it is constructed in symbolic shapes for the purpose of ceremonies. It is often related to the concept of the center, a portal through which the power of the gods and ancestors can be accessed.

The third related pattern shared by oral religions is respect for origins, gods, and ancestors. Origin stories describe how the world and the tribe came into being. While a High God is often acknowledged in oral religions, the primary focus is on gods or spirits most often associated with the forces of nature. Ancestors can exert a force over the present for good or ill, depending on how they are treated. They are regarded both with love and with respect for their power. Rituals are the basic means for creating harmony with the gods or spirits, ancestors, and nature. They are also a significant aid in making transitions between stages in the life cycle. Taboos help regulate social life and maintain religious order. When broken, they often require some sort of sacrifice. The shaman acts as an intermediary between the ordinary world and the spirit world. Utilizing trance states, shamans access the spirit world to gain powers of healing or insight to benefit the people. Finally, art objects or practices such as dance have a religious function and utilize the language of symbol.

Though many aspects of the modern world are threatening the practice of oral religions, some are experiencing a resurgence in their native cultures. Oral religions, beyond their immediate sphere, have influenced the ecological movement and music composers and artists around the world.

FILL IN THE BLANK

1. The sacred pipe used by many native peoples of North America is called a _____.

2. The _____ is the one who contacts the spirit world and attempts to manipulate the power of the spirits for one's tribe or group.

3. A strong social prohibition is called _____.

4. _____ is an animal or image of an animal that is considered related to a family or clan and is its guardian or symbol.

5. The act of pouring a liquid as an offering to a God is called a _____.

6. An organic, integrated system greater than the sum of its parts is _____.

7. _____ is the term for belief that everything in the universe is somehow alive.

8. Inspired by oral religions, Harvard biologist E. O. Wilson proposes that we foster biophilia, a _____.

9. The circle is sometimes symbolic of nature and its processes. Black Elk, an Oglala Sioux, points this out in reference to the circular tents of his people called _____.

10. The attempt through trance states to look into the past and future is known as _____.

MULTIPLE CHOICE

1. A bias against the study of oral religions up until the twentieth century is
   a. that too much variety exists.
   b. the idea that religious art should be impermanent.
   c. the assumption that they are not complex.
   d. that they contain too many taboos.

2. In the worldview of animism,
   a. there are no clear boundaries between the natural and the supernatural.
   b. definite boundaries exist between the natural and the supernatural.
   c. animals were once human beings.
   d. the natural world is superior to the supernatural.

3. To believe that nature is full of spirits implies that
   a. ghosts inhabit the world.
   b. human beings must treat all things with care.
   c. one must worship nature.
   d. one must fight with the spirits.

4. Sacred time is
   a. always moving forward and future-oriented.
   b. a time for formal worship.
   c. cyclical, returning to its origins for renewal.
   d. linear and focused on the present.

5. Constructed sacred space
   a. is never as effective as its natural counterpart.
   b. is a means of conforming daily life to mythic events.
   c. must be established near a striking natural site.
   d. is often in a symbolic shape such as a circle or square.

6. Oral religions
   a. make little distinction between a god and an ancestor.
   b. make a significant distinction between a god and an ancestor.
   c. often focus on a High God.
   d. usually worship androgynous deities.

7. Key events in the life cycle are
   a. taboo in many oral religions.
   b. marked with special rituals.
   c. dedicated to the ancestors.
   d. downplayed in tribal cultures.

8. The Native American vision quest is an example of
   a. a marriage ceremony.
   b. a girl's reception into the tribe.
   c. a rite of passage.
   d. assisting the spirit of a dead person to move on.

9. Taboos that have been broken are often mended through
   a. wearing masks for prescribed periods of time.
   b. dance and music.
   c. rites of passage.
   d. sacrifices.

10. The term *medicine man* refers to
    a. the keeper of the sacred pipe.
    b. missionary doctors who visit tribes.
    c. the chief of the tribe.
    d. the shaman.

11. Navaho sand paintings are
    a. a lost tribal art.
    b. etched into the sides of cliffs in the southwest.
    c. temporary creations in a ritual.
    d. used when other materials are unavailable.

12. A place where one can sometimes escape punishment is
    a. the underworld.
    b. a sanctuary.
    c. the abode of the ancestors.
    d. a tiki.

13. A common symbol signifying the center of the universe in many oral religions is
    a. the sacred tree of life.
    b. a lightning bolt.
    c. the feather.
    d. the good luck charm.

SHORT-ANSWER STUDY QUESTIONS, BY CHAPTER SECTIONS

Discovering Oral Religions

Where are some places oral religions are located? What accounts for the extensive variety found in these religions? (pp. 31–32)

Past Obstacles to the Appreciation of Oral Religions

1. List some of the reasons for the lack of attention by scholars toward oral religions. (p. 32)

2. What are some of the ways indigenous religions have expressed themselves artistically? (p. 32)

The Modern Recovery of Oral Religions

Describe some of the factors that have contributed to the modern study of oral religions. (pp. 33–34)

Studying Oral Religions: Learning from Patterns

Human Relationships with the Natural World

1. Why are human relationships with nature crucial for tribal and small-scale cultures? (p. 35)

2. Explain key features of the animistic worldview. (pp. 35–36)

3. Explain the "ethic of restraint" regarding nature that is frequently found in native religions. (pp. 36–37)

4. Why is it difficult for many people today to experience fully the intimate connection with the rest of nature? (p. 37)

Sacred Time and Sacred Space

1. Define sacred time in oral religions and give an example. (pp. 37–38)

2. What is sacred space and what is its relationship to the center? (pp. 37–38)

3. What features or actions establish sacred space? (p. 38)

Respect for Origins, Gods, and Ancestors

1. What is the purpose of origin stories and how are they expressed? (p. 38)

2. Describe concepts of a High God and lesser deities in oral religions. (pp. 38–39)

3. Why are gods and ancestors important? (pp. 42–43)

4. What concepts of an afterlife are found in oral religions? (pp. 42–43)

Religion of the Pueblo Peoples

1. Describe the region inhabited by the Pueblo peoples and the three great periods of development. (Box: pp. 40–43)

2. Discuss the role of guardian spirits and dance for Pueblo peoples. (Box: pp. 40–43)

Dogon of western Africa

1. What functions do the three religious societies of the Dogon perform? (Box: pp. 46–47)

2. Discuss the role of masks, animals, wooden figures, and Dogon temple architecture. (Box: pp. 46–47)

3. What has been the impact of outside influences (Islam and Western culture) on the Dogon? (Box: pp. 46–47)

Sacred Practices in Oral Religions

What is the purpose of ritual in oral religions? (p. 44)

Life-Cycle Ceremonies

1. Define "rites of passage" ceremonies and offer examples of key times in the life cycle when they occur. (p. 45)

2. Explain the purpose and methods of the vision quest common to many Native American religions. (pp. 45, 48)

Taboo and Sacrifice

1. What are taboos and why are they necessary? (p. 49)

2. List several taboos that regulate social behavior, both in oral religions and in modern society. (pp. 49, 52–54)

3. What actions are taken when a taboo is broken? (pp. 52–53)

Traditional Hawaiian Religion

1. Describe the triangle of islands that encompass Polynesian culture. (Box: pp. 50–52)

2. Name some of the key gods and goddesses of the Hawaiian religion and their attributes. In what forms might the gods or deceased ancestors appear to a person? (Box: pp. 50–52)

3. Discuss the role of a *kahuna,* or religious specialist, and the concept of *mana,* or spiritual power. (Box: p. 52)

Shamanism, Trance, and Spiritual Powers

1. What features form the essence of the shamanic mission? (pp. 54–55)

2. How do animals figure into the shaman's job? (p. 54)

3. Describe the theme of psychological death and rebirth in becoming a shaman. (p. 54)

4. Describe some of the roles a shaman often occupies in a tribal society. (p. 54)

5. What are some of the ways shamans induce the trance state? (pp. 54–55)

6. Explain the role and purpose of sympathetic magic and divination in native African religions and their Caribbean offshoots. (pp. 56–57)

Artifacts and Artistic Expression in Oral Religions

1. How do oral religions view art objects differently than modern secular culture views them? (p. 58)

2. Discuss the roles of dance, chants, masks, and carvings in oral religions. (pp. 58–60)

3. Explain the associations and symbolism of feathers and featherwork in many oral religions. (pp. 60–61)

Halloween: Fun or Folk Religion?

Discuss the origins and elements of oral religions found in Halloween, Christmas, or Easter. (Box: p. 61)

Oral Religions Today

1. Explain the four threats oral religions face today. (pp. 64–66)

2. How are oral religions surviving and even thriving in some locations today? (p. 66)

POSSIBLE PAPER TOPICS

1. Choose a specific oral religion and research it in depth according to the major themes introduced in the chapter. If it is one practiced in your area, attempt to meet with practitioners and incorporate summaries of the interviews in your paper.

2. Research the history, rich symbolism, and role of the sacred pipe in the religious life of many Native Americans.

3. Explore the role of an art form such as dance or the making and use of masks in an oral religion of your choice.

4. Discover in greater detail the role of religious societies among the Zuni of the American Southwest or the Dogon of western Africa.

INTERRELIGIOUS COMPARISONS

1. Explore the blend of Christian elements and features of oral religions in the Native American Church.

2. Compare Navaho religion of the American Southwest with Tibetan Buddhism. Anthropologist Peter Gold, *Navaho & Tibetan Sacred Wisdom: The Circle of the Spirit*, has written a fascinating account with abundant illustrations of similarities in sand paintings and mandalas, healing rituals, creation stories, cosmology, and psychology.

REFLECTION EXERCISES

1. People today generally do not experience the intimate connection with nature, and especially with animals, that is so important to oral religions. Except for household pets, many people experience animals only in zoos, on TV, or in cellophane packages in the meat department. Yet our language reflects an earlier time when animal traits and characteristics, or "powers," were readily attributed to people. Consider such phrases as "lion-hearted," "foxy lady," "wise as an owl," and "strong as an ox." Make a comprehensive list of these references and the characteristics to which they refer. Then contemplate the many connections between human and nonhuman species. This exercise may lead you to a research paper on the symbolism and important role of animals among indigenous peoples.

2. In oral religions, symbolic items or certain ritual actions protect or empower a person. One place this feature of oral religions shows up is in the phenomenon of good luck charms. Interview your friends to assemble a list of items that function in this capacity. Also consider the ritual actions some sports figures perform before or during games to ensure success.

3. What has been your most significant rite of passage? Were the rituals, whether religious or secular in nature, meaningful to you? Why or why not?

4. Have you ever experienced a place that seems particularly special or sacred? Consider places both in nature and in buildings. What contributes to your feeling about these locations?

ANSWERS

Fill In the Blank

1. calumet
2. shaman
3. taboo
4. Totem
5. libation
6. holistic
7. Animism
8. love of life
9. tipis
10. divination

Multiple Choice

1.	c	8.	c
2.	a	9.	d
3.	b	10.	d
4.	c	11.	c
5.	d	12.	b
6.	a	13.	a
7.	b		

CHAPTER 3

HINDUISM

LEARNING OBJECTIVES

After reading this chapter, you should be able to

♦   describe the origins of Hinduism.

♦   explain a monistic worldview.

♦   discuss concepts of karma, rebirth, and liberation.

♦   discuss aspects of social life, such as caste and stages of life.

♦   explain the practices and goals of the four religious paths.

♦   describe features of devotional Hinduism practiced by the majority of Hindus.

♦   recall the names and characteristics of Hinduism's most popular gods.

CHAPTER SUMMARY

The varieties of Hinduism began over four thousand years ago with a sophisticated civilization that was invaded by aggressive Aryan tribes who brought their own religious and social ideas. Vedic religion honored many gods and centered around priests performing sacrifices using fire and sacred chants. During the Axis Age, serious questioning, philosophic inquiry, and religious experimentation produced the Upanishads. These works record insights into external and internal spiritual reality (Brahman and Atman) that can be directly experienced through certain practices. Brahman stands for a monistic outlook that sees one invisible and subtle essence or source of all reality—human, divine, and cosmic. All is ultimately one. Behind, within, and beyond all multiplicity is Brahman. Atman is the innermost spirit within all human beings, which ultimately is identical with Brahman. Maya reflects a sense of magic and mystery and accounts for the perception of different forms or multiplicity in the world. Maya hides or veils the underlying unity of all things.

Karma and rebirth are important aspects of the Hindu worldview. Justice is built into the very fabric of reality. The moral consequences of one's actions will be experienced in this life or the next. Moksha represents the idea of final liberation or freedom from all limitations, especially the round of death and rebirth. Moksha entails going beyond egoism and identifying with the unity and sacredness that everything shares. The mysticism and abstractness of the Upanishads is balanced with practical religious elements that form the everyday spirituality of most Hindus. This synthesis is exhibited in the Bhagavad Gita. One should first strive to meet one's social obligations. Then the Gita recommends four paths, or yogas, that take into account one's caste and personality type. The paths of knowledge, action, devotion, or meditation may be practiced either individually or in combination.

The predominantly rural population of India follows a path of devotion that is centered around temples, home altars, pilgrimages, festivals, prayer, offerings, and hymn singing. A multiplicity of deities are available. But most people focus devotion on one particular god, whether male, female, or with features of androgyny. Hindu tolerance is based on the idea that all gods are really expressions of a single divine reality.

Other characteristics of Hinduism include the importance of the guru, a saintlike spiritual teacher and counselor who discloses his or her divine nature more fully than ordinary people. Animals also have a different status than in the West. They emerge from the same divine source as humans and may become human in future lives. Several gods have animal features or close animal companions.

Abstract religious themes such as multiplicity and unity are expressed in art through such media as stone and metal sculpture and instrumental music. Extensive symbolism is used both in painting and in sculpture. Dance and devotional music evoke religious emotions and more spiritual states of consciousness. The rich culture and religion of India is responding to challenges of the modern world and its conflict with Islam in many ways. Also, through its philosophies and such practices as yoga and meditation, and by producing such influential people as Gandhi, Hinduism is exerting an influence on the world far beyond mother India.

FILL IN THE BLANK

1. Nonviolence or nonharm is called _____.

2. A spiritual teacher who often has many followers is called a _____.

3. A _____ is a word or short phrase often chanted or used in meditation.

4. _____ is a spiritual discipline or practice for attaining union with the divine.

5. Such figures as Rama and Krishna are called _____, meaning the earthly embodiment of a deity.

6. A spiritual community where devotees live and study is called an _____.

7. Devotional practices to a deity or teacher fall under the heading of _____.

8. The moral law of cause and effect that governs one's rebirth is called _____.

9. The great literary work about Krishna that explains the four paths is _____.

10. The state of complete inner peace emerging in the deepest meditation is called _____.

MULTIPLE CHOICE

1. One feature that probably contributed to the rich developments in Hinduism was
   a. the constant invasions of India by foreigners.
   b. the frequent floods and fires across India.
   c. India's isolation from other areas.
   d. India's extensive natural resources.

2. Aryan religion was
   a. patriarchal and polytheistic.
   b. matriarchal and polytheistic.
   c. monotheistic.
   d. monistic.

3. The earliest sacred texts of Hinduism are the
   a. Upanishads.
   b. Brahmanas.
   c. Aranyakas.
   d. Vedas.

4. The second-ranking caste consisted of
   a. priests.
   b. merchants.
   c. nobles and warriors.
   d. artisans.

5. In the Bhagavad Gita, Krishna counsels Arjuna to
   a. meditate to experience moksha.
   b. work unselfishly for others.
   c. go to war.
   d. engage in nonviolent resistance.

6. Hinduism as formulated in the Upanishads
   a. encourages meditation to understand the essence of reality.
   b. says we must honor our social obligations and roles.
   c. rejected the authority of the Vedas in formulating new religious insights.
   d. advocates devotion to any of the many gods.

7. The Trimurti speaks of
   a. creation, fall, and salvation.
   b. gods, goddesses, and animals.
   c. creation, preservation, and destruction.
   d. death, rebirth, and liberation.

8. The most complicated of the Hindu gods is
   a. Vishnu.
   b. Rama.
   c. Shiva.
   d. Brahma.

9. The power of a god is often symbolized with
   a. lightning bolts.
   b. rings of fire.
   c. animals.
   d. many arms.

10. Respect is shown to gurus through
    a. an offering of food.
    b. touching their feet.
    c. memorizing sacred texts.
    d. bowing the head.

11. In the four stages of life, students and enunciates are
    a. to be celibate.
    b. to make pilgrimages to religious sites.
    c. to serve in temples.
    d. to care for the cows that wander the streets.

12. The most significant outside influence on Hinduism came from the
    a. Germans.
    b. Mongolians.
    c. Portuguese.
    d. British.

13. One of the qualities seen in the Brahman nature is
    a. the Feminine Divine.
    b. joy or bliss.
    c. jealousy.
    d. love.

SHORT-ANSWER STUDY QUESTIONS, BY CHAPTER SECTIONS

The Origins of Hinduism

1. What features of geography might have contributed to Hindu religious sensibilities? (pp. 73–74)

2. Explain one of the analogies of comparison that the author uses to understand Hinduism (a great river or a palace added to over centuries). Both convey the idea that nothing is ever lost in Hinduism. (p. 74)

3. What features have enabled Hinduism to develop freely in many directions? (p. 74)

The Earliest Stage of Indian Religion

What is noteworthy about the ancient Harappa culture? (pp. 74–75)

The Aryans and Their Religion

1. Describe the Aryans, according to origin and culture. (pp. 76–77)

2. What were the chief features of Aryan religion? (pp. 76–77)

The Vedas

Briefly describe the content or focus of the Vedas. (pp. 77–78)

The Upanishads and the Axis Age

What were some of the questions posed during this period? (p. 78)

Brahman and Atman

1. Define the term Brahman and relate an illustration from the Upanishads seeking to explain it. (pp. 80–81)

2. Explain what is meant by Atman and discuss its relationship to Brahman. (pp. 81–82)

Maya

1. How does maya fit into the Upanishadic explanation of the world? (p. 82)

2. Why is death not a tragedy, according to the Upanishads? (p. 82)

Karma

1. Explain the relationship between karma and rebirth. (p. 83)

2. Discuss the benefits and liabilities of embracing such a view as karma and rebirth. (p. 83)

Moksha

1. Describe the different aspects of liberation contained in the goal of moksha. (pp. 83–84)

2. How does kindness to all and detaching oneself from pleasure and pain relate to the attainment of moksha? (pp. 83–84)

Living Spiritually in the Everyday World

The Bhagavad Gita

1. Describe the general setting or plot of the Bhagavad Gita. (p. 84)

2. How have Gandhi and others interpreted the call to war in the Gita? (p. 86)

The Caste System

1. How is the caste system justified or explained in the Gita? (pp. 86–87)

2. Briefly describe the five main social classes found in India. (p. 87)

The Stages of Life

Highlight the four stages of life shaped by the ancient upper-caste ideal. (pp. 87–88)

The Yogas

1. Why are there different types of yoga? (p. 88)

2. Summarize the goals and viewpoint of jnana, or knowledge, yoga. (p. 89)

3. Besides stressing activity, what is of key importance in karma, or action, yoga? (p. 90)

4. Describe the various ways one can practice bhakti, or devotion, yoga. (p. 90)

5. Describe some of the types of meditation found in raja, or royal, yoga. (p. 91)

6. Describe the goals of kundalini yoga. (p. 91)

Hindu Meditation

Why do you think that Patanjali's eight steps necessary for meditation begin with ethical practices (self-control)? (Box: p. 90)

Devotional Hinduism

1. Why have intensive study and the practice of meditation had limited appeal for the majority of Hindus? (p. 92)

2. How is bhakti, or devotional, yoga expressed in daily life? (pp. 92–93)

The Trimurti: Brahma, Vishnu, and Shiva

1. Which major gods constitute the Trimurti and what interlinked forces do they represent? (p. 93)

2. How is Brahma portrayed and why might he be less popular in devotional Hinduism? (p. 93)

3. Convey the major features or stories of either Rama or Krishna, two of the avatars of Vishnu. (p. 94)

4. Discuss some of the significant features associated with Shiva. (pp. 94–96)

Worship of the Divine Feminine: Devi

1. Describe features of one of the popular goddesses in Hinduism, or how the Great Mother is worshiped. (p. 98)

2. Explain the concept of a female consort of a deity. (p. 98)

The Guru as Object of Devotion

1. Discuss the role and significance of a guru in Hindu spirituality. (p. 99)

2. Why do Hindus believe that one need only be in the presence of a guru to gain benefits? (pp. 99–100)

Devotion to Animals

1. Account for the kindness to animals displayed in Hinduism. (pp. 100–101)

2. Why does the cow receive special consideration? (p. 101)

Other Forms of Religious Devotion

What role do pilgrimage and festivals occupy in common religious expression? (pp. 101–102)

Hinduism and the Arts

1. Give some examples of multiplicity within Hindu art and explain their purpose. (p. 104)

2. How does Hinduism use symbolism in art? (pp. 105–106)

Hinduism: Modern Challenges

1. Summarize the relationship between Hinduism and Islam in India. (pp. 106–107)

2. Highlight the historical appeal of Islam in India. (p. 107)

3. What beliefs and practices were challenged through the British presence? (pp. 107–108)

Mohandas Gandhi

1. What were the influences that shaped Gandhi's philosophy? (pp. 108–109)

2. Highlight the key ideas and methods employed by Gandhi. (pp. 109–110)

Contemporary Issues

1. Discuss the current status of untouchables and the caste system. (p. 110)

2. How has the role of women changed through time? (pp. 110–111)

3. What are the sources of conflict between Hindus and Muslims? (p. 111)

4. Describe contemporary values most often associated with the West that are causing tension with India's traditional values. (pp. 111–112)

Hindu Influence beyond India

1. Where are some of the areas outside India where Hinduism is practiced? (p. 112)

2. Discuss the four waves of Hindu influence in the West. (pp. 113–115)

POSSIBLE PAPER TOPICS

1. Research and write in greater depth about Gandhi and the impact he had on both India and the larger world.

2. Explore a major period in Hinduism, such as the medieval period that produced great devotional literature and poetry.

3. Research the seven chakras, or centers, that are said to exist along the spinal column. Much has been written on this topic, including scientific and psychological research done in the West.

INTERRELIGIOUS COMPARISONS

1. Review characteristics of oral religions and trace their manifestations in Hinduism. This is something that can be done with most of the religions you will study.

2. Compare and contrast the role of sacrifice in Hinduism with that found in a religion of your choice. You will need to research how the concept of sacrifice has developed in Hinduism from Vedic times.

3. Explore the similarities and differences between devotional Hinduism and Christian piety. You also might compare certain beliefs such as *avatar* and incarnation and practices like the *puja* and communion.

REFLECTION EXERCISES

1. Hinduism offers as one explanation for its many gods that humans need concrete representations of the formless absolute. Also, finite minds can perceive the infinite only in a limited way, according to taste and temperament, cultural background, and other factors. Religions such as Christianity or Judaism view God in carefully defined ways that restrict the names and personality that reflect the divine. Yet even here, the way that God is pictured varies. Reflect on the images you have had of the divine, and interview friends about images they have had. How have these pictures in your mind changed since you were a child? Is it possible they will continue to change as you age or as you study religion deeper? How do you account for this process, and how would you attempt to measure the correctness of one image over another?

2. Hindu artists have used symbolism extensively to portray qualities of the divine. Some of this symbolism is universal, whereas other aspects emerged from their culture during different periods of history. Make a list of attributes you consider to belong to the divine. Then imagine how you would symbolize these characteristics using features from the modern environment.

3. The ancient Vedic priests used fire in their sacrifices, and as the author points out, fire still has significance to Hindus today. Fire is something that has been universally experienced by all peoples. It has been important in human life in many ways down through history. Therefore it often appears in religious symbolism in many different religions. Place the word "fire" in the center of a circle, and then on spokes coming out of the circle, list all the varied ways humans have used or experienced fire. Then reflect on how these attributes or uses of fire could express spiritual concepts or experiences.

ANSWERS

Fill In the Blank

1. ahimsa
2. guru
3. mantra
4. Yoga
5. avatars
6. ashram
7. bhakti
8. karma
9. the Bhagavad Gita
10. samadhi

Multiple Choice

1. c
2. a
3. d
4. c
5. c
6. a
7. c
8. c
9. d
10. b
11. a
12. d
13. b

CHAPTER 4

BUDDHISM

LEARNING OBJECTIVES

After reading this chapter, you should be able to

♦ describe the life story of the Buddha according to tradition.

♦ describe aspects of Hinduism that he rejected.

♦ explain the content of the Four Noble Truths.

♦ discuss concepts of change and no self in Buddhism.

♦ discuss the spread of Buddhism from India.

♦ distinguish between the three major branches of Buddhism.

♦ discuss Zen and its unique expressions in art.

CHAPTER SUMMARY

Buddhism began with the experience of one person during a time of religious ferment in India during the fifth century B.C.E. Born the son of a prince in what is now Nepal, Siddhartha Gautama forsook the life of a noble to seek spiritual answers to life's deepest questions, especially those concerning the profound suffering and eventual death all people experience. After much seeking and studying, Siddhartha had an enlightenment experience while meditating and took as his name the Buddha, the awakened one. He spent the rest of his life traveling to teach his insights and way of life.

His teachings were both practical and profound. He advocated a "middle path" between a worldly life and the extreme asceticism popular among religious seekers in India. He organized his teachings as the Four Noble Truths, which taught how to minimize suffering and attain inner peace. The First Noble Truth explored the reality and depth of suffering. The Second Noble Truth related suffering to desires or wants that were insatiable. The Third Noble Truth maintained that suffering could be eliminated by removing desire. The Fourth Noble Truth described how this could be done by following a path with eight aspects centering around the three main goals of seeing life objectively, living kindly and ethically, and cultivating inner peace through mental discipline and meditation. Contained in his teaching was the insight that the world is in constant change. Everything is made up of parts, and both the things and their parts are in such constant change that nothing, including personal identity, has permanence.

As a reformer, the Buddha rejected many aspects of the Hinduism of his day. These included the caste system, an emphasis on ritualism, elaborate metaphysical philosophizing, and belief in a permanent spiritual reality. He accepted ideas on karma and rebirth and the notion of liberation, which he called nirvana. In the centuries after his death, several schools emerged that finally crystalized into the great branches of Buddhism recognized today: Theravada, Mahayana, and Vajrayana.

Theravada is the only surviving conservative school whose goal was to pass on the Buddha's teachings unchanged. Theravada Buddhism centers on the interdependence of the community of monks with the laity. Monks pursue nirvana supported by the laity, who provide them with food, clothing, and provisions for the monastic life. Monks, in turn, are role models who run schools, meditation centers, and medical clinics.

The Mahayana branch subdivided into many different schools and introduced innovations in philosophy and practice. Sometimes these were logical developments or extensions of Buddhist ideas. They were often justified by appealing to secret teachings of the Buddha. The Mahayana ideal was the deeply compassionate person called a bodhisattva, who refused to fully enter nirvana to help others end their suffering. The historical Buddha was deemphasized in many schools by a worldview that saw the universe populated by many Buddhas and bodhisattvas. Major schools include Shingon, Tendai, Pure Land, Nichiren, and Zen.

Vajrayana is associated with Tibetan Buddhism that combines Mahayana principles with various esoteric practices incorporating mantras, mudras, and mandalas. An interesting feature is the transmission of leadership through reincarnations of other lamas.

FILL IN THE BLANK

1. One of the Three Jewels, _____ is the sum total of Buddhist teachings about how to view the world and how to live properly.

2. Another one of the Three Jewels, _____ is the community of monks and nuns.

3. _____ is the Buddha of the Western Paradise who by his merit allows people to be reborn in the Pure Land.

4. In Mahayana, someone of deep compassion who vows to not enter nirvana for the purpose of helping others is called a _____.

5. _____ is the Buddhist term meaning suffering, sorrow, or misery.

6. In Zen Buddhism, a _____ is a question that cannot be answered logically and is used to bring awakening.

7. Achieving _____, one gains inner peace and release from suffering and rebirth.

8. A text, especially one said to be the words of the Buddha, is called a _____.

9. The word for constant rebirth and its accompanying suffering is _____.

10. The virtue or quality of compassion or empathy is _____.

MULTIPLE CHOICE

1. The Buddha's name comes from a Sanskrit word meaning
   a. spirit warrior.
   b. middle path.
   c. the enlightened one.
   d. to wake up.

2. The Buddha's first disciples were
   a. his wife and child.
   b. his five former ascetic companions.
   c. the great King Ashoka.
   d. members of the warrior-noble caste.

3. According to the Buddha, his teachings must be
   a. accepted on faith.
   b. experienced in order to be worthwhile.
   c. memorized and chanted.
   d. spread by missionaries.

4. The Buddha was silent on questions about
   a. suffering.
   b. violence.
   c. inner peace.
   d. topics that were unanswerable.

5. Once a person reaches nirvana,
   a. suffering continues only for this life.
   b. samsara is attained.
   c. rebirth is finished.
   d. the Pure Land is entered.

6. Which did the Buddha *not* oppose?
   a. strong devotion to a guru
   b. the power of a priestly class
   c. detachment
   d. rituals for the gods

7. A sign of connection between Theravada monks and the wandering Hindu ascetics is
   a. the umbrella.
   b. the shaved head.
   c. the designation of being an arhat.
   d. the orange robe.

8. Zen is derived from a word referring to one of the steps in the Eightfold Path, whose meaning is
    a. compassion.
    b. wisdom.
    c. to live kindly.
    d. meditation.

9. Mahayana Buddhism generally does not advocate
    a. devotion to deities.
    b. use of elaborate ritual.
    c. individuals trying to enter nirvana.
    d. speculation on unanswerable questions.

10. Mahayana Buddhism
    a. spread south to Ceylon and east to Thailand.
    b. continued in India until modern times.
    c. spread north to China and Japan.
    d. replaced Taoism in China.

11. Each Dalai Lama in Tibetan Buddhism is considered to be
    a. the Buddha reincarnated.
    b. King Ashoka reincarnated.
    c. an emanation of the bodhisattva Avalokiteshvara.
    d. an emanation of Amitabha.

SHORT-ANSWER STUDY QUESTIONS, BY CHAPTER SECTIONS

The Beginnings of Buddhism: The Life of the Buddha

1. Describe the social context of India in Siddhartha Gautama's day. (pp. 120–121)

2. Give a brief outline of the Buddha's life, according to the legends. (pp. 121–125)

3. Describe the Buddha's death and his last advice to his disciples. (p. 125)

The Basic Teachings of Buddhism

1. What is meant by the Buddha's "noble silence"? (p. 125)

2. What were the two most important questions about existence on which the Buddha concentrated? (p. 126)

The Three Marks of Reality

1. Explain the dimensions of change that the Buddha saw in the world. (p. 126)

2. How does Buddhism explain the concept of no permanent identity? (p. 127)

3. Discuss the meaning and scope of suffering in Buddhism. (pp. 127–128)

The Four Noble Truths

1. Explain in your own words the phrase "to live is to suffer." (p. 128)

2. Discuss dimensions of desire found in the Second Noble Truth. (pp. 128–129)

3. How does individualism contribute to suffering? (p. 129)

4. What degree of enlightenment might a layperson hope to attain in this life? (pp. 129–131)

The Noble Eightfold Path

Relate the eight steps of the path to its three main goals. (p. 131)

The Influence of Indian Thought on Early Buddhist Teachings

What facets of Indian Vedic practice did early Buddhist literature reject? (p. 131)

Ahimsa: "Do No Harm"

Discuss the reasons that Buddhists embrace an ethic of nonharm. (pp. 132–133)

The Soul and Karma

How does Buddhism explain karma and rebirth without a soul? (p. 133)

Nirvana

Discuss your understanding of nirvana in Buddhism. (pp. 133–135)

"Who am I?"

Review how different cultures and religions would answer this question, then focus on the Buddhist response and the reasons for it. (Box: p. 134)

Was the Buddha an Atheist?

1. What are the two questions implied within the larger question of the existence of God? (Box: p. 135)

2. What was the Buddha's position on those two questions? (Box: p. 135)

The Early Development of Buddhism

1. Discuss Ashoka's conversion to Buddhism. (pp. 135–137)

2. What actions are attributed to Ashoka that aided the spread of Buddhism? (p. 137)

Theravada Buddhism: The Way of the Elders

1. What has been the goal of Theravada regarding Buddha's teachings? (p. 138)

2. Describe the importance of the community of monks for Theravada. (pp. 138–139)

3. What countries have been influenced by Theravada Buddhism? (p. 139)

4. How do monks and laity serve each other? (pp. 139–140)

5. Discuss some of the unique features of Buddhism in Thailand. (Box: p. 140)

Theravada Teachings and Literature

Briefly describe the topics covered in the "three baskets." (pp. 140–141)

Theravada Art and Architecture

1. Describe some of the symbols used in the early centuries to represent Buddhism. (pp. 141–143)

2. What were some of the common poses of the Buddha when images of him began to be used? (p. 143)

Mahayana Buddhism: The "Big Vehicle"

1. What have been some of the criticisms within Buddhism of the Mahayana branch? (p. 143)

2. How have the criticisms of Mahayana Buddhism been answered? (p. 143)

New Ideals: Compassion and the Bodhisattva

1. Explain the logic behind the compassion in the Mahayana perspective. (pp. 143–144)

2. What is a bodhisattva? (p. 145)

3. Discuss the concept of "skillful means" in Mahayana. (p. 145)

Mahayana Thought and Worldview

1. Briefly explain the trikaya, or "three-body" doctrine. (p. 146)

2. What is the role of Maitreya, the future Buddha, and how has he been pictured or envisioned? (pp. 146–147)

3. Who are the heavenly bodhisattvas and what do they do? (p. 147)

4. Explain the doctrine of shunyata, or emptiness. (p. 148)

5. Explain what is meant by tathata, or "suchness," and how it is experienced. (p. 149)

Mahayana Literature

What are some of the key ideas in the Mahayana texts? (p. 149)

Mahayana in China

1. Discuss Mahayana features that appealed to the Chinese. (p. 152)

2. Discuss the Buddhist values and practices that conflicted with Chinese ideals. (p. 152)

Some Major Schools of Mahayana

1. Why do Mahayana sects show such a wide variety in attitudes toward uses of art, ritual, and the pursuit of worldly success? (pp. 155–156)

2. What were the goals and practices of Shingon? (p. 156)

3. How did the Tendai school deal with the profusion of Buddhist texts and teachings? (p. 158)

4. Describe the beliefs and practices of Pure Land Buddhism and name the Buddha of their devotion. (pp. 158–159)

5. Who is Nichiren and what did he proclaim? (pp. 159–160)

Zen Buddhism: Enlightenment through Experience

1. Describe the Taoist values that paved the way for Chan, or Meditation school, Buddhism in China. (pp. 160–161)

2. Discuss the views of the northern school and the southern school regarding enlightenment. (p. 161)

3. Describe the content of the satori experience. (p. 161)

Zen Techniques for Enlightenment

1. Describe the practice of zazen, or sitting meditation. (p. 163)

2. What is the purpose of a koan? (p. 163)

3. Explain the value of manual labor as a Zen technique. (p. 163)

Buddhism and the Arts of Japan

Discuss how one of the arts such as haiku, tea ceremony, ceramics, ikebana, garden design, or calligraphy reflects Zen values. (pp. 163–167)

Buddhist Festivals

Relate aspects of a Buddhist festival of your choice. (Box: p. 153)

Vajrayana Buddhism: The "Diamond Vehicle"

Discuss meanings of the name "diamond" or "lightning bolt" vehicle. (p. 167)

Origins, Practice, and Literature of Tibetan Buddhism

1. How did Padmasambhava reconcile the native Bon religion with that of Buddhism? (pp. 168–169)

2. Describe some of the basic features that were blended together to form Tibetan Buddhism. (p. 169)

3. How did the "Yellow Hat" sect begin? (pp. 169–170)

4. How does the transmission of leadership occur in Tibetan Buddhism? (p. 170)

Ritual and the Arts

1. Discuss the symbolism of the ritual objects of the vajra and bell. (p. 170)

2. What is the purpose of a prayer wheel or prayer flag? (p. 171)

3. Briefly define mudras and mandalas. (p. 172)

4. Who is the Dalai Lama and how has his influence spread outside Tibet? (pp. 173–175)

Buddhism, the West, and Modern Challenges

1. What are some of the qualities of Buddhism that have been attractive to people in the West? (pp. 175–176)

2. How has Buddhism influenced Western painting, poetry, and literature? (p. 177)

3. Briefly outline the four historical waves of interest in Buddhism in the West. (p. 177)

4. What is the origin and focus of the so-called fourth vehicle of Buddhism? (p. 178)

5. What challenges or attacks has Buddhism faced in its traditional home countries? (p. 178)

6. In what ways is Buddhism experiencing a resurgence in the East? (p. 178)

POSSIBLE PAPER TOPICS

1. Research in depth one of the arts influenced by Buddhism. Connect expressions of that art with Buddhist themes and practices.

2. Focus on one of the Buddhist branches or schools in depth. Try to connect your findings with the basic themes of Buddhism discussed in this chapter.

3. Explore a controversial ethical issue like euthanasia or abortion from a Buddhist perspective.

INTERRELIGIOUS COMPARISONS

1. Compare Shinran's ideas about salvation by grace alone to those of Martin Luther in Protestant Christianity.

2. Compare and contrast Buddhist notions of nirvana with the Hindu concept of moksha.

3. Trace shamanistic themes or influences in Tibetan Buddhism.

REFLECTION EXERCISES

1. The core teachings of the Buddha express something universal about human experience. Reflect on specific experiences you have had or witnessed in others that illustrate the Four Noble Truths. Recount specific elements of the Eightfold Path that reduced or eliminated the suffering.

2. The concept of no-self is perhaps the most difficult idea in Buddhism. Besides its philosophical justification, it is related to the phenomenon of suffering, with which we all have experience. Once while teaching that part of Buddhism in a Comparative Religions course, I was experiencing some kind of misery in my personal life. In an experiment, I decided to take a Buddhist approach. When I was feeling down, rather than saying to myself "I feel hurt and I am sad," I said "There is hurt and sadness." To my surprise, the emotional intensity decreased. I was identifying and witnessing mental and emotional phenomena as they appeared, without directly attaching it to the little "me" inside. Try it yourself sometime!

3. Thich Nhat Hanh is a Buddhist originally from Vietnam. He has introduced the verb *inter-be* to reflect interrelationships and interdependencies. Consider an object of your choice, such as a loaf of bread, and trace all the ways that object is connected to or dependent on forces or things outside itself. If you removed those forces, could the object still exist? It seems like the bread or whatever object you choose *inter-is* with just about everything else.

4. Many people cannot see the point in being detached or in feeling neutral to both pleasant and unpleasant things in the world. But sometimes the Buddhist logic is inescapable. Consider your feelings toward your favorite food. When that food becomes leftovers, after a few weeks you would not want to eat it! The same food becomes garbage, and we have quite different feelings toward it. Yet the garbage can be composted, and then enrich the soil so that good food is once again produced. Doesn't it seem rather strange to have such different emotional reactions to the different aspects of this natural process?

ANSWERS

Fill In the Blank

1. dharma
2. sangha
3. Amitabha
4. bodhisattva
5. Dukkha
6. koan
7. nirvana
8. sutra
9. samsara
10. karuna

Multiple Choice

1.	d	7.	d
2.	b	8.	a
3.	b	9.	a
4.	d	10.	c
5.	c	11.	c
6.	c		

CHAPTER 5

JAINISM AND SIKHISM

LEARNING OBJECTIVES

After reading this chapter, you should be able to

♦   discuss the origins of Jainism.

♦   describe the key beliefs and ethical practices of Jainism.

♦   discuss similarities and differences between Jainism, Buddhism, and Hinduism.

♦   describe the emergence of Sikhism in India.

♦   explain the key beliefs and values of the Sikhs.

♦   discuss similarities and differences between Sikhism, Hinduism, and Islam.

CHAPTER SUMMARY

Jainism and Sikhism emerged at different times in India and share certain characteristics with Hinduism, such as a belief in karma and rebirth. Each took divergent paths and developed in opposition to certain Hindu views or practices, and each represents a move toward greater religious simplicity. Jainism emerged as a historical religion about the same time as Buddhism with the appearance of Mahavira. He is said to be the twenty-fourth great person or, "crossing maker," to reach perfection in the present cycle of the universe. Mahavira's life story has many parallels with the Buddha's. Both engaged in extreme asceticism and practiced meditation that led to an experience of liberation from bondage to the ordinary world.

Jainism explicitly rejects belief in a creator-God or in the possibility of receiving blessings from higher beings. It sees the universe as eternal but continually changing and going through regular great cycles of rise and fall. All parts of the universe are composed of both spirit and matter, and everything is full of life and is capable of suffering. Human beings are unique in their awareness of their dual nature and can overcome limitations and bondage of the material world and the body through insight, austerities, and kindness. Jains practice five ethical recommendations that are adjusted to particular life situations. Profound nonviolence, or *ahimsa,* is the foundation of Jain ethics, which also include nonlying, nonstealing, chastity, and nonattachment. Jains seek to purify themselves and perfect their characters. They see all life as a preparation for the liberation of the spirit from the body, and so have often valued an intentional "holy death" at the end of a long life of virtue and detachment.

Sikhism emerged in the fifteenth century in a region of India with a long history of conflict between Hindus and Muslims. It began with Nanak's powerful religious experience of the oneness of God beyond all human names and conceptions. He believed Hindus and Muslims really worshiped the same God, which he simply called the "True Name," which signified that all names and terms applied to God are limited. Nanak and his friend Mardana traveled throughout northern India preaching and seeking converts. Nanak blended Hindu and Muslim elements in his clothing, composed and sang devotional songs, and preached strong social responsibility as a religious obligation. Nanak disdained Hindu polytheism and devotion to images of various gods and goddesses. He taught that God was beyond personhood, yet had personal qualities such as knowledge, love, a sense of justice, and compassion.

Sikhs revere ten gurus, beginning with Nanak and ending with Gobind Singh. The final, permanent guru is believed to contain the living spirit of Nanak and his successors. It is the Adi Granth, the sacred book of the Sikhs that contains hymns and poems composed by the gurus and saints. Responding to Muslim persecutions during the time of the gurus, the Sikhs became increasingly militant. Gobind Singh began a special military order called the Khalsa that was open to all castes. Today Sikh males are recognized by the five practices originally adopted by the Khalsa. These include uncut hair and beard, hair comb, special underwear signifying willingness to fight at a moment's notice, the sword, and a bracelet of steel. Sikhs are known for their values of self-reliance, strength, and endurance. Worship services are held in temples that are open to non-Sikhs. The most famous is the Golden Temple of Amritsar, a popular Sikh pilgrimage site.

FILL IN THE BLANK

1. The spirit or soul that enlivens matter is called _____.

2. Matter without soul or life is called _____.

3. _____ is the belief that all physical matter has life and feeling.

4. A perfected person in Jainism who will not be reborn is a _____.

5. In Jainism, _____ refers to one of the twenty-four ideal human beings of the past. Its literal meaning is _____.

6. The last and greatest of the twenty-four who reached perfection is _____.

7. The founder of Sikhism was _____.

8. The primary scripture of the Sikhs is the _____.

9. The Golden Temple of the Sikhs is located in the city of _____.

10. The special military order founded by Gobind Singh was called the _____.

MULTIPLE CHOICE

1. The most accurate descriptor of Jainism is
   a. polytheistic.
   b. monotheistic.
   c. atheistic.
   d. nontheistic.

2. Jains, unlike the Theravada Buddhists,
   a. reject monastic disciplines.
   b. glorify Mahavira's extreme austerities.
   c. believe in karma and reincarnation.
   d. advocate ahimsa.

3. Jains, like the Theravada Buddhists,
   a. believe that all attachments bring a certain bondage.
   b. have the same ethical requirements for monks and laity.
   c. value a holy death.
   d. became a thriving merchant class.

4. In his lifetime, Mahavira taught and
   a. organized an order of naked monks.
   b. preached one God against Hindu's polytheism.
   c. admitted nuns to the monastic order.
   d. became a Vedic priest.

5. After a long life of virtue and detachment, Jains endorse
   a. intensive meditation.
   b. compassionate action for the poor.
   c. self-starvation.
   d. that one become a guru.

6. Regular practices of the Jains include
   a. almsgiving and animal sacrifice.
   b. fasting and pilgrimage.
   c. deity worship and meditation.
   d. wearing orange or white robes.

7. Both Jainism and Sikhism
   a. practice vegetarianism.
   b. advocate ahimsa.
   c. are monotheistic.
   d. view the human being as a composite of spirit and matter.

8. Sikhism originated in the
   a. northeastern part of India close to where Buddhism began.
   b. Punjab of northwestern India and eastern Pakistan.
   c. southern part of India.
   d. lake region of India.

9. The most accurate meaning of the Sikh term *gurdwara* is
   a. guru.
   b. temple.
   c. military guard.
   d. holy war.

10. The meaning of the word *sikh* is to
    a. preach and seek disciples.
    b. fast and engage in confession.
    c. perform devotional acts.
    d. meditate.

11. Nanak's religious experience is similar to what feature in other religions?
    a. enlightenment
    b. mystical union
    c. prophetic call
    d. ceremonial purification

12. The Sikh Khalsa adopted the five practices to
    a. promote strength and self-identity.
    b. combine elements of Hinduism and Islam.
    c. remember the lineage of gurus and saints.
    d. attain mystical consciousness.

13. Members of the Khalsa are to avoid
    a. sexual relations.
    b. violence.
    c. growing beards.
    d. intoxicants.

SHORT-ANSWER STUDY QUESTIONS, BY CHAPTER SECTIONS

Shared Origins

Offer some general comparisons and contrasts between Jainism and Sikhism. (p. 186)

Jainism—Background

Describe some features Jainism shares with Buddhism. (p. 187)

Mahavira and the Origins of Jainism

1. What is some of the symbolism behind the image of the twenty-four tirthankaras? (p. 187)

2. Discuss the traditional life story of Mahavira. (pp. 187–188)

Worldview

1. What are the philosophic arguments Jainism uses to defend its atheism? (p. 189)

2. How does Jainism conceive time? (p. 189)

3. Explain the dualism found in Jainism and how it shapes understanding of human beings. (pp. 189–190)

4. How are human beings different from other things composed of matter and spirit? (pp. 189–190)

5. Discuss the Jain goal and the understanding of karma and rebirth. (p. 190)

6. What role do superhuman beings occupy in Jainism? (p. 190)

Jain Ethics

1. Explain *ahimsa* and how this ethical recommendation is lived out. (p. 190)

2. Briefly describe the ethical recommendations of nonlying, nonstealing, and chastity. (p. 191)

3. Discuss the importance of nonattachment for Jains. (p. 192)

4. Explain how a "holy death" fits into the Jain religion. (Box: p. 192)

The Development of Jainism and Its Branches

1. Discuss similarities and differences between Buddha and Mahavira. (pp. 192–193)

2. What beliefs distinguish the Digambara branch? (p. 193)

3. What features distinguish the Shvetambara branch? (p. 193)

4. Describe the beliefs of the Sthanakavasi branch. (pp. 193–194)

5. What features characterize the reformist Terapanthis branch? (p. 194)

Jain Practices

1. How do Jains understand the role of devotional practices? (p. 194)

2. Describe the basic features of a Jain puja. (p. 194)

3. Name some key Jain pilgrim sites. (p. 195)

Jain Scriptures

Describe some of the general contents of Jain canonical and noncanonical scriptures. (pp. 195–196)

Jain Art and Architecture

How are the features of Jain statues interpreted? (pp. 196–197)

Sikhism—Background

1. What are some of the chief differences between Hinduism and Islam? (p. 197)

2. What are the few things Hinduism and Islam share? (p. 197)

Nanak and the Origins of Sikhism

1. What was Nanak's revelation and how did it occur? (pp. 197–198)

2. How did Nanak convey his teachings? (p. 198)

The Worldview and Teachings of Nanak

1. Describe features of Hinduism that Nanak accepted. (pp. 198–199)

2. Which characteristics of Hinduism did he reject? (p. 199)

3. What was Nanak's teaching about God? (p. 199)

The "Five K's" of the Sikh Khalsa

Briefly describe the five practices originally adopted by members of the Khalsa. (Box: p. 201)

The Development of Sikhism

1. What defines the earliest stage of Sikhism? (p. 199)

2. Describe important features of the second stage of consolidation and religious definition. (pp. 199–201)

Sikh Scriptures

1. What is the general content of the three parts of the Adi Granth? (p. 201)

2. How is the Adi Granth viewed and treated? (p. 201)

3. Describe various ways the Adi Granth is used. (pp. 201–202)

Sikhism and the Modern World

1. Describe the dislocations and antagonisms experienced by Sikhism. (pp. 202–203)

2. Where have Sikhs established communities and attracted converts outside India in its third and final stage of development? (p. 203)

POSSIBLE PAPER TOPICS

1. Research in depth the contributions of each of the ten Sikh gurus.

2. Explore *ahimsa* in Jainism and study how Gandhi applied it to modern times.

3. Research the modern struggle of Sikhism to establish a separate state in India.

INTERRELIGIOUS COMPARISONS

1. Compare and contrast the purpose and the practice of Jain and Hindu puja devotions.

2. In greater depth, compare and contrast Sikhism with either Islam or Hinduism.

3. The sword is an important symbol in Sikhism with great historical significance. In Japan, the sword became historically and symbolically significant in certain schools of Zen Buddhism. Compare and contrast this fascinating role of the sword in religion.

REFLECTION EXERCISES

1. The Jains honor twenty-four great people, or *tirthankaras,* who serve as heroes and role models. Most religions have saints or special people that accomplished extraordinary things. Even outside the sphere of religion, people have mentors and role models. Who are the people who have most influenced you? They can be people you know personally or famous figures from the past. After compiling the list of those who are great people for you, ponder the characteristics you most admire about them. How could you develop these attributes in your own life?

2. Both Jainism and Buddhism claim certain jobs are not appropriate for anyone on a spiritual path. For the Jains, that would be any occupation that inflicted harm even on animals. Consider life today. Can you identify any occupations that you think conflict with a spiritual path? What are your reasons?

3. Jains and many Hindus maintain home altars. Many other religious traditions do likewise, including Orthodox Christianity and some Roman Catholics. These altars are a reminder of one's religious commitment and identity. They serve as a call to devotion. Many believe their homes are blessed by these altars. Perhaps this same impulse manifests in the secular world of work, where people set aside part of their desk or office for personal items and pictures of those closest to them. What personal items have you placed around your work or study area? What do these objects mean to you? If you were to intentionally establish a home altar, what would be on it?

ANSWERS

Fill In the Blank

1. jiva
2. ajiva
3. Hylozoism
4. jina
5. tirthankara, crossing-maker or ford-finder
6. Mahavira
7. Nanak
8. Adi Granth
9. Amritsar
10. Khalsa

Multiple Choice

1. c
2. b
3. a
4. a
5. c
6. b
7. d
8. b
9. b
10. a
11. c
12. a
13. d

CHAPTER 6

TAOISM AND CONFUCIANISM

LEARNING OBJECTIVES

After reading this chapter, you should be able to

♦ describe the basic elements of traditional Chinese belief that appear in later developments of Chinese religions.

♦ relate basic details of the lives of the key founders of Taoism and Confucianism.

♦ define the meaning of Tao.

♦ discuss Taoist values and ideals, and the images used to convey them.

♦ discuss the focus and goals of Confucianism, especially in terms of the Five Great Relationships, the Confucian Virtues, and the notion of the "noble person."

♦ describe how Taoism and Confucianism shaped Chinese arts.

CHAPTER SUMMARY

Ancient China, before the great religions emerged, already saw patterns in nature, had concepts of yin and yang, venerated the ancestors, and had other beliefs associated with the Chinese way. Over the centuries, both Taoism and Confucianism developed these ideas further but in different directions.

The Taoists, beginning with Laozi (Lao Tzu), spoke cryptically about nature and its operation and what it meant to live harmoniously with the Tao, the principle or power that makes the universe move through the patterns and rhythms seen in nature. The Taoists saw the veneer of civilization as something artificial or at least far removed from the Tao, the source of all. Disdaining formal education, they advocated a more intuitive path best conveyed through stories or in images such as water. Simplicity, gentleness, humility, and a certain earthiness were Taoist values. Yet this apparent ordinariness also embodied a different way of looking at the world and being in it. Taoists sought a special effortless way of acting to accomplish one's purposes, longevity, and often the attainment of extraordinary powers.

Confucius focused on human fulfillment in the social sphere of life, for surely the Tao flowed through the human world just as it did in nature. Troubled by the political turmoil and what he perceived as a decline in civilization, Confucius advocated a program of comprehensive education and the cultivation of special virtues. He wanted both to develop individuals who could be social leaders and to create a harmonious society. He appealed to tradition and the past as a model for the present. In Confucian thinking, to a great extent human beings are their relationships. So careful attention to the duties and obligations of a person's different relationships with others was a central focus. One must live up to the highest expectations or standards of the various social roles one occupied, beginning with the family.

The superior or noble person would have an inner integrity and a deep consideration for others. This person would have mastered the social graces—all those countless rituals of propriety that allow for smooth interaction between people. The noble person would avoid extremes in life, maintaining equilibrium and harmony. Additionally, the aesthetic sense would be developed, manifested in a love for all the arts associated with civilization, such as poetry and literature, calligraphy, painting, and music. By automatically choosing to do what is right after years of practice and study and by fulfilling one's job duties and social obligations properly, one would be united with the force of the universe.

Despite changes brought by the Communists, Confucian values continue to influence not only China but all of East Asia. They include attention to family and social harmony while observing a hierarchy in both family and society; a respect for the aged; and the valuing of education and self-discipline. Confucian and Taoist values have shaped the arts of China. Ultimately, the two are seen to be complementary, with Confucianism dominating the social realm and Taoism informing one's private life.

FILL IN THE BLANK

1. The Taoist term for no strain or effort is _____.

2. In Taoist thought, the term for the unnameable origin of the universe and the way nature expresses itself is _____.

3. _____ is the receptive aspect of the universe, expressing itself in silence, darkness, and rest.

4. _____ is the active aspect of reality, expressing itself in speech, light, and movement.

5. The _____ is the classic scripture of Taoism, known for its brevity and poetic paradox.

6. The book of the sayings of Confucius is called the _____.

7. _____ is the Confucian virtue embracing the arts and cultural refinement.

8. _____ is the Confucian virtue meaning appropriate action, protocol, ritual, or etiquette.

9. _____ is the Confucian virtue meaning consideration for others and is written in the Chinese ideogram of "person" and "two."

10. The Confucian ideal or noble person embodying all the virtues was called _____.

MULTIPLE CHOICE

1. In the most famous picture of Laozi (Lao Tzu), he rides
   a. a horse.
   b. a pedicab.
   c. an ox.
   d. a donkey.

2. According to the traditional story, Laozi wrote down his teachings only because
   a. a border guard would not let him pass until he did so.
   b. his students and disciples begged him.
   c. a request came from Confucius.
   d. he needed money.

3. According to the Taoists, if one leaves behind desires for individual things, one will
   a. die.
   b. be reborn to a better life.
   c. see things differently.
   d. become nameless.

4. Which is not a Taoist value?
   a. simplicity
   b. spontaneity
   c. sensing movements of nature
   d. formal education

5. In Zhuangzi's (Chuang Tzu's) famous dream, he was not certain that he was not
   a. Confucius.
   b. an ox.
   c. a butterfly.
   d. a Taoist.

6. Taoists view death as
   a. a great evil.
   b. a predictable transformation of nature.
   c. an offering to the ancestors.
   d. necessary for one's next rebirth.

7. By his teachings, Confucius hoped to
   a. counter the influx of Buddhism into China.
   b. produce virtuous people and create a harmonious society.
   c. make a break with the past and focus China on the future.
   d. draw people closer to Tian (Heaven).

8. Confucius thought the most important relationship was
   a. ruler-subject.
   b. husband-wife.
   c. father-son.
   d. friend-friend.

9. Which was not an additional virtue endorsed by Confucius?
    a. loyalty
    b. emotional control
    c. thrift
    d. pride

10. To a great extent in Confucianism, people are
    a. selfish and need strict guidelines.
    b. naturally good and best left alone.
    c. individuals first.
    d. their relationships.

11. For Confucius, a person who follows the way of heaven
    a. avoids extremes and remains in harmony with others.
    b. lives close to nature.
    c. may be a great warrior.
    d. is always meek and humble.

12. The most liberal thinkers in ancient China were
    a. the Legalists.
    b. the Taoists.
    c. the Confucians.
    d. followers of Xunzi.

13. The main thrust of the Cultural Revolution was to
    a. renew and reform Confucianism.
    b. stamp out the last vestiges of capitalism in China.
    c. break with the past and all that was antiquated.
    d. install the Communists as the new leaders of China.

SHORT-ANSWER STUDY QUESTIONS, BY CHAPTER SECTIONS

Basic Elements of Traditional Chinese Beliefs

Highlight some of the elements of early Chinese belief that provided the basis for later developments in Chinese religions. (pp. 208–211)

Taoism—The Origins of Philosophical Taoism

1. Describe the style and focus of the Tao Te Ching. (pp. 213–214)

2. What does it mean to say that the Tao is nameless? (p. 214)

3. Explain the meaning of some of the images that express the Tao. (pp. 214–215)

4. Relate a story told by Zhuangzi (Chuang Tzu) and its meaning. (pp. 215–217)

The Basic Teachings of Philosophical Taoism

1. Define *wu wei* and give an example. (p. 218)

2. Explain what Taoists mean when they advocate simplicity, gentleness, and relativity. (p. 218)

Taoism and the Quest for Longevity

Describe some of the Taoist techniques for extending the life span. (pp. 218–219)

Religious Taoism

Describe some of the concerns and practices of religious Taoism. (pp. 219–221)

Taoism and the Arts

1. How is perspective used in Chinese nature painting and what Taoist sensibilities are expressed by it? (p. 224)

2. What role does empty space play in nature painting? (p. 224)

3. Name some themes of Chinese poetry that are valued by Taoists. (pp. 224–226)

4. How do Chinese house and garden design express the balance of yin and yang? (p. 226)

5. Discuss the Chinese view of nature and its impact on people as manifested in the Chinese garden. (p. 226)

Taoism and the Modern World

Describe where Taoist influences are felt today. (p. 226)

Confucianism—The Tao in Confucianism

Contrast the views of Confucianism and Taoism regarding the Tao. (pp. 227–228)

The Life of Confucius

Recall some of the basic features of Confucius' life. (pp. 228–229)

Living According to Confucian Values

1. What were the two central goals or ideals embraced by Confucius? (p. 229)

2. Describe the Confucian ideal person or "excellent" human being and how you would recognize one. (Box: p. 230)

3. Explain why Confucius thought education was so important. (p. 229)

4. What are the Five Great Relationships according to Confucius and why do so many of them deal with the family? (pp. 230–233)

5. Explain what Confucius meant by "the rectification of names." (p. 233)

The Confucian Virtues

    1. List the Five Confucian Virtues and briefly define them. (pp. 234–236)

    2. Describe other virtues stressed by Confucius. (p. 237)

Confucian Literature

    1. What role or function has the Confucian canon played in Chinese history? (p. 237)

2. Summarize the scope and concerns of Confucian literature. (Box: p. 238)

The Development of Confucianism

Schools of Philosophy

Describe some of the schools of philosophy that were in competition with Confucianism. (pp. 238–241)

The Development of Confucianism as a Religious System

1. Describe the ways Confucianism responded to the Buddhist challenge. (pp. 241–242)

2. Highlight the main features of the Neo-Confucianism movement. (p. 243)

Confucianism and the Arts

1. Why is calligraphy the premier Confucian art form? (pp. 244–245)

2. In what ways did Confucianism influence painting? (p. 246)

3. How would you describe both the moral and the civilizing aspects of art? (pp. 246–248)

Confucianism and the Modern World

1. Summarize the Communist criticism of Confucianism. (p. 249)

2. How are Confucian values thriving in East Asian countries? (p. 250)

3. How might Confucianism be modified in its next stage? (p. 251)

POSSIBLE PAPER TOPICS

1. Though Taoism, Confucianism, and Buddhism all emphasize peace and nonviolence, aspects of the three contribute to the philosophy behind Asian martial arts. Investigate some of the connections, which will vary in the different martial arts.

2. Explore the history of one of the Chinese arts and how it was influenced by either Taoism or Confucianism.

3. Examine the resurgence of Confucianism in an Asian country of your choice.

INTERRELIGIOUS COMPARISONS

1. Compare the concept of the Tao with the Brahman of Hinduism.

2. Investigate the main tenets of an organization like Promise Keepers, analyzing them from a Confucian perspective.

REFLECTION EXERCISES

1. Wu wei is the Taoist concept of spontaneous and effortless action. One manifestation of it occurs at special times in repetitive activities like running, when the thinking mind is at rest and there are no concerns about pushing harder or winning or losing. All tension is absent, and one is especially in tune with the body and the environment. Movements are precise and intuitive, and one is unaware of chronological time. The Taoists maintain that this is all quite natural and that this kind of awareness can be cultivated in various ways. Everyone has experienced such moments at one time or another. Explore your own experiences of such times and interview friends or family members for theirs.

2. The Confucian virtue of li attends to propriety and ritual. Think of all the ways human beings have ritualized the social intercourse of daily life. Actually it may be more difficult to find a mode of social interaction that is not ritualized in some way. Examine the simple rituals of greeting one another. Isolate the components of intent, word, and gesture. When does the ritual work and when does it not? Then investigate something more complicated, like the rituals of dating. Explore the value of clearly defined rituals in this area versus a more Taoist approach of freedom and spontaneity. Which do you prefer and why? If the previous "either/or" question bothers you, then you may already be thinking with a Chinese-like mind. If so, try combining the two approaches in a yin/yang way.

3. If you can relate to Zhuangzi's dream about not being sure if he was a butterfly dreaming he was a Chinese philosopher or the other way around, then you probably have some Taoist sensibilities. Have your dreams ever had a special meaning? Or what about that curious time somewhere between wakefulness and sleep when your mind wanders freely? Mostly we dismiss these experiences and get about the tasks facing us each day. But the Taoists see things differently and come to value what most others frequently overlook. Can you see any worth or meaning in attending to these experiences?

4. Zhuangzi used whimsical stories to express Taoist themes and values. Try your own hand at creating such a story.

ANSWERS

Fill In the Blank

1. wu wei
2. Tao
3. Yin
4. Yang
5. Analects
6. Tao Te Ching
7. Wen
8. Li
9. Ren (jen)
10. junzi (chun-tzu)

Multiple Choice

1. c
2. a
3. c
4. d
5. c
6. b
7. b
8. c
9. d
10. d
11. a
12. b
13. c

CHAPTER 7

SHINTO

LEARNING OBJECTIVES

After reading this chapter, you should be able to

♦ retell portions of the Shinto creation story.

♦ explore the tensions and accommodations between Shinto, Buddhism, and Confucianism.

♦ describe the focus and practice of Shinto.

♦ discuss the contributions of Shinto to Japanese culture and history.

♦ describe characteristics of the New Religions that are Shinto offshoots.

♦ discuss the features of Shinto that make it relevant to the modern world.

CHAPTER SUMMARY

As an oral religion in its ancient beginnings, Shinto had no known person or group as its founder, focused on living harmoniously with nature, and had unique creation stories and elements of shamanism. The heart of Shintoism is centered on the kami, who are the spirits that animate nature and govern its rhythms. They are associated with such features as trees, rivers and waterfalls, the ocean, and mountains. The kami also include gods and goddesses, animal spirits, and ancestors who have become kami. Because kami are everywhere and have power to influence human life, they must be treated with reverence. Homage is paid by visiting them at their shrines and by maintaining harmony with nature and its processes.

The moral philosophy of Shinto is twofold: First, one must behave respectfully toward spirits, human beings, and nature. Second, one must perform proper rituals of purification, cleanliness, and reverence. Shinto is silent on controversial ethical questions and lets the individual decide. Toward humans, one must honor obligations, be sincere, and not be egotistical. Mistakes can be corrected with apologies and repaid debts. Shinto regards human beings and the world as good. The focus is on blessings in this life, such as new life and fertility, health, and wealth.

Shinto was forced to define itself with the introduction of Buddhism from China in the sixth century. Over the years there was a blending and accommodation with Shinto and both Buddhism and Chinese Confucianism. Buddhism was valued for its philosophy, help with serious illness, funerals, and the afterlife, whereas Shinto was associated with agriculture, fertility, and birth. Shinto shrines adopted certain Buddhist practices and Chinese architectural details. Buddhist temples often included Shinto shrines. Confucianism was more easily incorporated with its veneration of ancestors and emphasis on family and clan loyalties. Shinto came to reinforce Confucian values of respect for the emperor, care for juniors, self-discipline, and love of learning.

Shinto has provided a sense of national identity for the Japanese through its ancient practices and close ties to the land. Also attractive are mythological stories about the divine origin of the islands and of a people loyal to an emperor who was descended from the sun goddess. There is a felt sense of family with all members of the nation. When Shinto was nearly assimilated by Buddhism, priests demanded an independent Shinto. The movement eventually led to the Meiji Restoration in the nineteenth century. Thereafter Shinto served a growing spirit of nationalism and militaristic expansionism that culminated in World War II.

Shinto practices include shrine visits, blessings done by priests at the shrines and in the community, participating in festivals and seasonal holidays, especially New Years, water purifications, and making offerings and prayer at home shrines. Perhaps because of a lack of organizational structure, Shinto has generated an amazing variety of sects that often borrow from Confucianism, Buddhism, and even Christianity. Offshoots that consider themselves separate religions are called the "New Religions." Shinto's esteem for nature, its silence on most moral and doctrinal questions, its aesthetically pleasing rituals, and its eclecticism may have modern significance well beyond the shores of Japan.

FILL IN THE BLANK

1. A feudal warrior or soldier was called a _____.

2. The gatelike structure that marks a Shinto sacred space is a _____.

3. A spirit, god, or goddess of Shinto is known as a _____.

4. The term for a Shinto shrine is _____.

5. In Shinto mythology, the primordial female parent god is _____.

6. In Shinto mythology, the primordial male parent god is _____.

7. The goddess of the sun in Shinto mythology is _____.

8. The code of the warrior involving loyalty, duty, and self-sacrifice is _____.

9. The suicide fighter pilots of World War II were called _____.

10. Dramas associated with Shinto that are performed in mask and costume are called _____.

MULTIPLE CHOICE

1. According to Shinto mythology, the islands of Japan were created by
   a. a marriage between the sun and moon gods.
   b. tears from the primordial male parent god.
   c. brine dripped from a spear that had been stirred in the ocean.
   d. tears from the primordial female parent god.

2. Which of the following was not introduced from China?
   a. writing
   b. city planning
   c. concern with purity
   d. meditation techniques

3. The Japanese have relied on Shinto to
   a. help give them a sense of national identity.
   b. keep foreign influences out of Japan.
   c. moderate excessive patriotism.
   d. provide comforting funeral rites.

4. Shinto was used to promote war because
   a. its essence idealizes harmony and peace.
   b. it embodies the warrior code of bushido.
   c. its State Sect was too close to the government.
   d. Buddhism refused to support the war effort.

5. Shinto is concerned with all of the following except
   a. fertility.
   b. internal guilt.
   c. family values.
   d. animal spirits.

6. The kami of nature
   a. are one's ancestors.
   b. like to dwell in places of power and beauty.
   c. are the former emperors of Japan.
   d. are said to move around the islands of Japan.

7. People visit Shinto shrines to
   a. engage in formal meditation.
   b. stand under waterfalls.
   c. receive blessings at important times in their lives.
   d. see the shrine treasures.

8. Shinto priests routinely perform all of the following ceremonies except
   a. weddings.
   b. blessing homes.
   c. funerals.
   d. exorcisms.

9. Before the New Year's Celebration,
   a. formal visits are made to relatives and friends.
   b. the home must be thoroughly cleaned.
   c. a blessing must be received from the priest.
   d. one must visit a shrine.

10. Visitors to Shinto shrines often
    a. stand under waterfalls.
    b. wear long white robes.
    c. clap their hands.
    d. leave mirrors as offerings.

11. Sometimes visitors to shrines tie to a tree pieces of paper that have written on them
    a. their requests.
    b. the names of their children.
    c. important dates.
    d. confessions of wrongdoing.

12. Shinto has probably generated many offshoots because of its
    a. conflicts with Buddhism.
    b. emphasis on nature.
    c. silence on many ethical issues.
    d. lack of strong organizational structure.

13. The emperor of Japan traditionally has
    a. led pilgrimages to the shrine at Ise.
    b. been associated with Mt. Fuji.
    c. been the high priest of Shinto.
    d. balanced Shinto and Buddhism.

SHORT-ANSWER STUDY QUESTIONS, BY CHAPTER SECTIONS

The Origins of Shinto

1. What is the meaning of Shinto and when did this designation appear? (p. 256)

2. Briefly retell the Shinto creation myth. (pp. 256–257)

3. What features are found in the creation myth that are intriguing because they reflect Shinto values and concerns? (pp. 258–259)

The Historical Development of Shinto

What forces prompted Shinto to define itself? (p. 259)

Accommodation with Buddhism and Confucianism

1. What were the accommodations reached between Shinto and Buddhism? (pp. 259–260)

2. How did Shinto mesh with Confucian values? (pp. 260–261)

Shinto and Japanese National Identity

1. Highlight the details of the Meiji Restoration. (pp. 262–263)

2. Differentiate State Shinto from Sect Shinto. (p. 263)

3. Why did State Shinto end? (p. 263)

Kamikaze Pilots and Shinto

1. Who were the kamikaze pilots? (Box: p. 262)

2. What elements produced the warrior ideal of bushido? (Box: p. 262)

Essentials of Shinto Belief

1. What is at the heart of Shinto? (p. 263)

2. Explain who the kami are. (p. 263)

3. What is the morality that flows from the Shinto system of values? (p. 264)

4. Why does Shinto turn its focus away from death? (p. 264)

5. Discuss the role of washing or cleaning in Shinto. (p. 264)

6. Where are the kami located and how are they to be treated? (p. 264)

Shinto Religious Practice

Worship at Shrines

1. Why do people visit Shinto shrines? (p. 265)

2. Describe the features of the shrines. (pp. 265–266)

3. Describe the actions one performs when visiting the shrine. (pp. 266–267)

4. What sort of items are considered shrine "treasures"? (p. 266)

5. What functions do Shinto priests perform? (p. 268)

Celebration of the New Year

What sort of ritual actions are performed by Shinto followers during the New Year's Celebration? (pp. 268–269)

Observances of the Seasons and Nature

1. How do the seasons and nature factor into Shinto? (p. 269)

2. What other practices do some followers of Shinto perform to achieve purification and union with certain kami? (p. 269)

Other Practices

1. Describe daily worship at home for followers of Shinto. (pp. 269–270)

2. How is the emperor viewed in Shinto and what duties does he perform? (p. 270)

Shinto and the Arts

1. What are the defining features of Shinto concerning art? (pp. 272–273)

2. Why has Shinto lent itself to an appreciation of the beauty of ritual? (p. 273)

Architecture

1. Describe the features of shrines that reflect Shinto artistic expression. (p. 273)

2. What Chinese influences are seen in Shinto buildings? (p. 274)

3. What function do the *torii* serve? (p. 274)

Music and Dance

How are music and dance used in Shinto practice? (pp. 275–276)

Shinto Offshoots: The New Religions

1. Describe the strengths and weaknesses of Shinto not being a strongly institutionalized religion. (pp. 276–277)

2. What are the four general groups of sects and offshoots of Shinto? (pp. 277–278)

3. Describe some of the unifying features and concerns that characterize the New Religions. (pp. 277–278)

4. What might the New Religions show about the direction of religions in general in the future? (p. 278)

Shinto and the Modern World

Describe the four elements of Shinto that have particular modern significance. (pp. 278–279)

POSSIBLE PAPER TOPICS

1. Review the chapter on Oral Religions and select a few features by which to explore Shinto in depth.

2. If you explore one of the New Religions, identify elements borrowed from Shinto and other religions, or review the chapter on Understanding Religion and analyze the New Religion according to the key characteristics that define religion.

INTERRELIGIOUS COMPARISONS

1. Compare and contrast ideas about purity and uncleanliness between Shinto and Hinduism. After reading Chapter 8, you could also include Judaism.

2. Select one of the major periods in Japanese history and explore the complex interactions between Shinto, Buddhism, and perhaps Confucianism.

3. Religion has often, been used to justify war. Explore this history and its justification in Shinto and in a religion of your choice.

REFLECTION EXERCISES

1. In the chapter on Oral Religions, you may have reflected upon special places in nature that have meaning to you. Shinto also values such places that can actually become part of one's identity. Another idea Shinto could convey is that every place is unique and special (the kami are everywhere). Consider where you live now. What makes it special and unique?

2. Another related reflection is based on the idea that Oral Religions contain stories on how a particular people came to a place. Shinto has stories about the creation of Japan, how the first people got there, and the adventures that shaped them in this land. Consider where you now live. What brought you to this place and how has this place brought you to you?

3. Washing, sweeping, and cleaning have religious significance in Shinto. Reflect on how you feel after a shower or after you've cleaned and organized a room. From the Shinto perspective, the cleansing and self-discipline required is an exercise of purification. Relevant is the recommendation of some psychologists that to make a change in our inner lives it helps to make change in our outer lives. Also remember the phrase grandmothers used to be fond of saying, "Cleanliness is next to godliness."

ANSWERS

Fill In the Blank

1. samurai
2. torii
3. kami
4. jinja
5. Izanami
6. Izanagi
7. Amaterasu
8. bushido
9. kamikaze
10. Noh

Multiple Choice

1. c
2. c
3. a
4. c
5. b
6. d
7. c
8. c
9. b
10. c
11. a
12. d
13. c

CHAPTER 8

JUDAISM

LEARNING OBJECTIVES

After reading this chapter, you should be able to

♦ discuss developments in the four general periods of Jewish history.

♦ describe the three parts of the Hebrew Bible.

♦ retell some of the major stories in the Hebrew scriptures.

♦ describe Jewish religious practices.

♦ explain the characteristics of the major divisions within Judaism.

♦ discuss the history of persecution that culminated in the Holocaust.

♦ discuss challenges Judaism faces in the modern world.

CHAPTER SUMMARY

The history of the Jews can be divided into four periods of time that began with a homeless people called the Hebrews or Israelites. They eventually found a homeland in Israel marked with the milestones of establishing a kingly dynasty, a capital in Jerusalem, and a Temple. A second period began in the sixth century B.C.E. when the kingdom of Judah and its first Temple were destroyed and the people were forced into a fifty-year exile in Babylon. This event led to the emergence of the synagogue and prompted putting religious law and history in written form to guarantee its survival. After the exile, the work of the priests took on great significance. Influences from the surrounding cultures also began to enter into Jewish life and knowledge of Hebrew declined. With foreign domination came Zoroastrian ideas and later the appeal of Hellenistic culture. Tensions between accommodation and rejection of external influences led to the rise of religious factions after 165 B.C.E. These included the Sadducees, the Pharisees, the Zealots, and the Essenes, who possibly assembled the Dead Sea Scrolls. This period also saw the growth of the diaspora, Jewish communities outside the land of Israel.

The next period was initiated in the common era when the second Temple was destroyed by the Romans in 70 C.E. This ended the power of the priesthood, whose sacrificial rituals were no longer possible, and forced the religion to move toward a greater focus on scripture. The Hebrew canon was finalized and commentaries were written. Classical or rabbinic Judaism and traditional Jewish life were established, as was mystical Kabbalah. Great communities in the diaspora both flourished and endured persecution, mainly at the hands of European Christians. The final period, called the Reform, began in about 1800 as a response to the European Enlightenment. It was an impetus to question and modernize traditional Judaism, and it helped produce the diverse branches within Judaism today, which hold differing views on Jewish identity and practice. Centuries of persecution and dislocation reached a climax with the Holocaust under the reign of Adolf Hitler. One-third of all Jews were killed. Out of the ashes, the Nation of Israel was born.

Judaism is often associated with its most important book. The Hebrew Bible contains a variety of material that essentially records interactions and responses between the people and a God who is portrayed in complex ways, perhaps reflecting different ancient traditions that were ultimately combined. The scriptures are divided into three parts. First is the Torah, the sacred core of five books containing stories of the Creation, Adam and Eve, a Great Flood, the Hebrew patriarchs and matriarchs, and Moses, the great liberator and lawgiver. It includes laws about religious ritual and daily conduct, including the Ten Commandments. The second part is called the Prophets, after those people who spoke in God's name to the Jewish people. The third part is called the Writings, which include a variety of material, such as short stories, proverbs, poetry, and reflections on life.

Judaism centers on a way of life that recognizes the presence of God and the sanctification of human life. Beyond embracing the Ten Commandments, the most obvious examples are keeping the Sabbath, observing Holy Days and Festivals, and following dietary practices. The mythic power of its great stories and the clarity of its ethical codes have shaped Western civilization. Judaism is known for its strong moral orientation and a this-worldly focus that has led to major contributions in multiple fields.

FILL IN THE BLANK

1. The _____ were the priestly faction, influential during the Second Temple period.

2. The _____ refers to the dispersion of Jews beyond Israel.

3. _____ is the early winter festival celebrated with the lighting of candles for eight days.

4. The movement that has encouraged the creation and support of the Nation of Israel is called _____.

5. The _____ is the encyclopedic commentary on the Hebrew scriptures.

6. The special ritual meal at Passover that recalls the Exodus from Egypt is called the _____.

7. The Hebrew word for commandment is _____.

8. A _____ is a candlestick that usually contains seven branches.

9. The word meaning teaching or instruction that can refer to the first five books of the Hebrew scriptures is the _____.

10. A _____ is a Jewish teacher or minister.

MULTIPLE CHOICE

1. The Hebrews trace themselves to an ancestor named
   a. Adam.
   b. Abraham.
   c. Abel.
   d. Noah.

2. A contract between the Hebrews and their God was called a
   a. mitzvah.
   b. covenant.
   c. yarmulke.
   d. commandment.

3. Someone inspired by God to speak for him was called a
   a. priest.
   b. rabbi.
   c. prophet.
   d. king.

4. God first appeared to Moses in
   a. an Egyptian slave.
   b. a cloud on Mt. Sinai.
   c. a burning bush.
   d. the Red Sea.

5. The sacred core of the Hebrew Bible is sometimes called the
   a. Pentateuch.
   b. Talmud.
   c. Writings.
   d. Prophets.

6. The first King of Israel was
   a. Daniel.
   b. Moses.
   c. David.
   d. Saul.

7. Who conquered the northern kingdom?
   a. the Babylonians
   b. the Persians
   c. the Assyrians
   d. the Romans

8. Who conquered the southern kingdom?
   a. the Babylonians
   b. the Persians
   c. the Greeks
   d. the Egyptians

9. The anti-Roman nationalistic Jewish faction that was active during the Roman period of control over Israel was the
   a. Pharisees.
   b. Sadducees.
   c. Zealots.
   d. Essenes.

10. The semi-monastic Jewish community during the Roman period that referred to themselves as the "sons of light" were the
    a. Pharisees.
    b. Sadducees.
    c. Zealots.
    d. Essenes.

11. Mystical speculation sometimes prompted by persecution was the
    a. Tanakh.
    b. Midrash.
    c. Kabbalah.
    d. Talmud.

12. The Jewish Day of Atonement is
    a. Ashenazim.
    b. Hanukkah.
    c. Passover.
    d. Yom Kippur.

13. The three centers of Jewish life today include Israel, the United States, and
    a. Morocco.
    b. Poland.
    c. Germany.
    d. Russia.

SHORT-ANSWER STUDY QUESTIONS, BY CHAPTER SECTIONS

An Overview of Jewish History

1. Why is the destruction of the Second Temple of Jerusalem a pivotal point in studying Jewish history? (p. 286)

2. What are the two periods that subdivide the time before the destruction of the Second Temple? (p. 286)

3. What are the two periods that subdivide the time after the destruction of the Second Temple? (p. 286)

The Hebrew Bible

1. Name the three sections of the Hebrew Bible and briefly describe the content of each. (p. 288)

2. What is the scholarly view regarding the exactness of the historical record depicted in the Hebrew Bible? (p. 289)

Biblical History

In the Beginning: Stories of Origins

1. Describe the key points made in the story of origin. (pp. 289–290)

2. Describe the highlights of the second origin account. (p. 291)

3. Who were Adam and Eve's children and what is notable about them? (p. 291)

4. Briefly retell the story of the Great Flood. (p. 291)

5. What was the purpose of the tower of Babel and what does the story explain? (p. 291)

6. What evidence in the scriptural text indicates the first eleven chapters of Genesis serve a non-historical, symbolic purpose? (p. 292)

The World of the Patriarchs and Matriarchs

1. Describe the call of Abraham and the promise made to him. (p. 292)

2. Briefly retell the story of Abraham and Isaac and give a possible meaning. (p. 292)

3. Define a theophany and give an example. (p. 293)

4. Describe the life of Joseph. (p. 294)

Moses and the Law

1. Why was the baby Moses cast adrift in a basket? (p. 295)

2. What is the case for the earliest Hebrews being polytheistic in outlook? (p. 295)

3. Describe the views of God in the two traditions in the Torah. (p. 296)

4. How did the Passover festival get its name? (p. 296)

5. Describe the events surrounding Moses' encounter with God at Mount Sinai. (pp. 296–297)

6. What is the meaning of a covenant? (p. 297)

7. What is the nature of the rules given after the Ten Commandments? (p. 297)

8. Describe the general content of the Books of Numbers and Deuteronomy. (p. 299)

9. Briefly state the first four of the Ten Commandments. (Box: p. 298)

10. Briefly state the rest of the Ten Commandments. (Box: p. 298)

The Judges and Kings

1. Describe the role of a judge after the time of Moses. (p. 299)

2. For what is King David noted? (p. 300)

3. Describe the accomplishments of King Solomon. (p. 300)

4. What caused the division into two kingdoms after Solomon's death? (p. 300)

5. How did one typically become a prophet? (p. 300)

6. How did prophets usually explain political losses suffered by the Hebrews? (p. 300)

7. List the empires that conquered the northern and southern kingdoms and give the dates. (p. 301)

Exile and Captivity

What significant changes occurred with the exile in Babylonia? (pp. 301, 304)

Return to Jerusalem and the Second Temple

1. Under what circumstances were the Jews allowed to return to their homeland? (p. 304)

2. What important accomplishments occurred in the period of the Second Temple? (p. 305)

Zoroastrianism

1. Describe the religious climate Zarathustra faced. (Box: pp. 302–303)

2. What was the content of Zarathustra's vision? (Box: p. 303)

3. What are the teachings contained in the Zoroastrian scriptures? (Box: p. 303)

4. Describe some of the Zoroastrian beliefs that may have influenced the Essenes, early Christianity, and Islam. (Box: p. 303)

5. What are some of the distinctive rituals practiced by Zoroastrians? (Box: pp. 303–304)

Cultural Conflict during the Second-Temple Era

The Seleucid Period

1. Describe the political realities Israel faced in the Seleucid Period. (pp. 305–306)

2. What were some of the cultural achievements and attractions of Hellenism? (p. 306)

Responses to Outside Influences

1. Who were the Sadducees and what were their views? (p. 306)

2. Describe Pharisee concerns. (p. 306)

3. What was the Zealot view? (p. 307)

4. Describe the practices and views of the Essenes. (p. 307)

5. What has been the significance of the Dead Sea Scrolls thus far? (p. 307)

The Development of Rabbinical Judaism

Describe the two major effects of the destruction of the Jerusalem Temple. (p. 309)

The Canon of Scripture and the Talmud

1. How does tradition describe the events that established the Hebrew scriptures? (p. 309)

2. What are some of the interpretive works that came after the formation of the canon? (p. 310)

Islam and Medieval Judaism

Why did Islam treat Jews with tolerance in the medieval period? (p. 310)

The Kabbalah

1. Describe some of the methods for interpreting scripture in Jewish mysticism. (pp. 311–312)

2. What are some of the mystical speculations found in Kabbalah? (p. 312)

Christianity and Medieval Judaism

1. Why did Christians persecute Jews? (pp. 312–314)

2. Describe the restrictions imposed on Jews by Christians in medieval Europe. (p. 314)

Questioning and Reform

1. What were some of the developments in the Renaissance that affected both Christianity and Judaism? (p. 314)

2. Explain the emphasis of Hasidism. (p. 314)

3. What did those Jews who stressed modernization advocate? (p. 315)

Judaism and the Modern World

What were some of the major persecution-driven migrations of Jews before World War II? (p. 315)

Hitler and the Holocaust

1. Describe Hitler's beliefs concerning racial classes and conspiracy theories. (pp. 315–316)

2. Review the scope of the Holocaust. (p. 317)

Creation of the State of Israel

What factors contributed to the creation of the state of Israel? (p. 317)

Jewish Belief

1. Though there is no official Jewish creed, what are the central beliefs formulated by the medieval scholar Maimonides? (p. 320)

2. What does it mean for human beings to be created in God's image? (p. 320)

3. How have Jews understood their special role among human beings? (p. 320)

Religious Practice

1. What is the goal of all laws by which Jews live? (p. 321)

2. Explain some of the unique practices of Jewish meditation. (Box: p. 321)

The Jewish Sabbath

Describe the purpose of the Sabbath and some of its observances. (p. 321)

Holy Days

1. What are the High Holy Days and how are they kept? (pp. 322–323)

2. Describe the celebration of Hanukkah and its origins. (p. 323)

3. Explain some of the features of the Seder meal observed during Passover. (p. 324)

Jewish Dietary Practices

What are the dietary practices and restrictions of traditional Judaism? (pp. 325–326)

Other Religious Practices

1. Describe the ritual of daily prayer as practiced by traditionalist males. (pp. 326–327)

2. What are the Jewish attitudes and practices surrounding sexuality? (p. 327)

Divisions within Contemporary Judaism

Culturally Based Divisions

1. Who are the Sephardic Jews? (p. 328)

2. Who are the Ashkenazic Jews? (p. 328)

3. What are some of the other smaller Jewish cultures? (pp. 328–329)

Observance-Based Divisions

1. What are some of the defining characteristics of Orthodox Judaism? (pp. 329–331)

2. How is Conservative Judaism characterized? (p. 331)

3. What are the features of Reform Judaism? (pp. 331–332)

4. Describe Reconstructionist Judaism. (p. 332)

The Contributions of Judaism

1. Describe some of the values embraced by Jewish culture. (pp. 332–333)

2. List briefly some Jewish contributions to the fields of philosophy, literature, psychology, and music. (pp. 333–334)

3. What has been the Jewish contribution to the film industry? (p. 335)

Jewish Identity and the Future of Judaism

Explain the difficulty in defining Jewish identity. (pp. 335–336)

POSSIBLE PAPER TOPICS

1. Research the many interpretations of the story of Adam and Eve.

2. Research the history, development, and major figures of either the prophets or the wisdom literature.

3. Choose a period in Jewish history and explore it in depth.

INTERRELIGIOUS COMPARISONS

1. The Jewish scholar Moses Maimonides argued that faith and reason were complementary. Roughly a half century later, St. Thomas Aquinas held the same position in the Christian world. Compare and contrast the reasoning of these two thinkers.

2. Tradition and ritual are very important in both Judaism and Confucianism. Compare and contrast the purpose and function in each.

3. How is the monotheistic vision of the Sikhs similar to and different from that of the Jews?

REFLECTION EXERCISES

1. Take the time to read in the Hebrew Bible some of the stories mentioned in the chapter. Many people are surprised to discover that the greatest Israelite heroes are portrayed in a very human way. They are not idealized saints, but flesh and blood people with distinct personalities. They possess both strengths and weaknesses that affect their lives and those around them in dramatic ways. Identify some of these traits and trace the lives of these people. With whom do you identify and with whom do you feel antagonism? This will say much about who you are.

2. Rent a video of the movie *Schindler's List* and perhaps watch it with a few friends or classmates. The movie chronicles the Nazi campaign against the Jews and evokes emotions ranging from horror and despair to hope and triumph. Reflect on the terror human beings can do to one another and on the depth of suffering and persecution experienced by the Jews. Also ponder the strength of the human spirit and the power of those who commit to life and goodness.

3. Consider Judaism's many festivals and holidays, each with a particular emphasis and practice. Observing these times with others creates a deep sense of belonging and a connection with an ancient tradition. These practices help shape identity and bring people to the realization that they are part of something much larger than themselves. Certainly, one cannot know what it is like to be part of a practicing Jewish community from the outside. But perhaps those of us on the outside might review celebrations and practices that serve a similar function in our lives. How could you enhance or develop them further? You might want to get one of the popular books on rituals for suggestions.

ANSWERS

Fill In the Blank

1. Sadducees
2. diaspora
3. Hanukkah
4. Zionism
5. Talmud
6. Seder
7. mitzvah
8. menorah
9. Torah
10. rabbi

Multiple Choice

1. b
2. b
3. c
4. c
5. a
6. d
7. c
8. a
9. c
10. d
11. c
12. d
13. d

CHAPTER 9

CHRISTIANITY

LEARNING OBJECTIVES

After reading this chapter, you should be able to

♦ summarize the life and teachings of Jesus, especially in the context of his times.

♦ describe the structure and content of the New Testament.

♦ explain Christian doctrines and practices.

♦ discuss the growth of Christianity.

♦ describe medieval and modern developments.

♦ explain the origins of the three major branches of Christianity.

♦ assess the impact Christianity has had on the arts.

CHAPTER SUMMARY

Christianity is centered around the person of Jesus. He was born during a time of great religious and political unrest in Israel under Roman domination. The Jews were splintered into groups that advocated widely divergent responses to the times. Many believed they were living in the "end times" and expected God to intervene in a dramatic way, which would include the appearance of a leader called the Messiah. Jesus' ministry of teaching and healing probably began in his late twenties and lasted no more than three years. He was arrested in Jerusalem at Passover time by authorities who considered him a threat. He was soon tried and executed by crucifixion on a cross. Three days after he was buried, his followers found an empty tomb. Others reported appearances and visitations by a transformed Jesus that had been resurrected from the dead. Christian scriptures say that forty days later he ascended to the heavens, promising to return again.

Virtually all we know of Jesus comes by way of the four Gospels in the New Testament that describe the life and teachings of Jesus. These portraits of Jesus were recorded some time after his death and reflect the distinctive viewpoints and culture of the individual writers. Jesus is portrayed as a Jew accepting the practices and authority of his tradition. Noted for independence of thought, Jesus centers his teaching on the subject of the Kingdom of God. He emphasizes love for God and other people. He recommends not judging others, compassion, help for the needy and oppressed, forgiveness, and nonviolence. He urges simplicity and is wary of overly strict observance of laws when they hurt people.

Paul is responsible for the spread of belief in Jesus beyond the Jewish world through his extensive travels, powerful letters, and incisive thinking. Through his prompting and leadership, the early church decided that converts did not have to observe Jewish religious laws. In Paul's view, a right relationship with God came only through faith in Jesus. Following moral rules was done willingly out of gratitude for what God had accomplished through Jesus' sacrifice on the cross. Essentially, Paul's views on the meaning of Jesus, morality, and Christian practice became the norm for most of the Christian world.

The Christian worldview took many centuries to be fully worked out through discussions, controversies, and great councils that produced the central creeds of the faith. The Holy Trinity is the belief that God, although one, is three "persons." The Father is the guiding intelligence that created the universe and made human beings an important part of the divine cosmic plan. The Son is Jesus Christ, who has both a fully human and a fully divine nature united in one person. The Holy Spirit is the power of God that guides all believers. Christians believe in life after death, a resurrection of all people, and a final judgment that will lead to an eternal life in either a joyous Heaven or a torturous Hell, depending on one's faith and goodness in the eyes of God.

In the Middle Ages, Christianity developed thriving monastic and mystical movements and produced great figures such as Francis of Assisi. Controversies over doctrine and church structure led to schisms that produced the great branches of Eastern Orthodox, Roman Catholic, and Protestant Christianity—with Protestantism itself subdividing many more times.

Christian practice is rich, complex, and varied in the different branches. All Christians practice Baptism and observe the Lord's Supper, with varying understandings. Holidays that mark significant times in the life of Christ and the early church, such as Easter and Christmas, are celebrated. Christianity has had a profound effect on the arts in the fields of architecture, painting, sculpture, and music. Its themes and stories are echoed in much great literature. Christianity continues to affect history and has in turn faced challenges from the modern world, especially with the growth of science and changing roles of women.

FILL IN THE BLANK

1. Correct belief or doctrine is called _____.

2. An _____ was one of Jesus' twelve disciples.

3. The Lord's Supper is referred to by the Greek word _____.

4. Essential belief or a system of beliefs is called _____.

5. An _____ is a religious painting on wood used in the Orthodox Church.

6. The doctrine of the _____ is the belief that God became visible in Jesus.

7. Disobedience to God is called _____.

8. The belief that the death of Jesus has paid the price of God's justice for all wrongdoing is called _____.

9. A _____ is an account of the life of Jesus, meaning literally "good news."

10. _____ is the belief that a human being's ultimate reward or punishment is already known to God and even caused by him.

MULTIPLE CHOICE

1. The term messiah means
   a. priest.
   b. angel of the Lord.
   c. Son of God.
   d. anointed.

2. For those who would turn Jesus into a champion and protector of the family, the gospel evidence is
   a. missing.
   b. mixed.
   c. solid.
   d. against this.

3. The most Jewish in orientation of the gospels is
   a. Matthew.
   b. Mark.
   c. Luke.
   d. John.

4. The gospel that is *not* part of the synoptics is
   a. Matthew.
   b. Mark.
   c. Luke.
   d. John.

5. The gospel sometimes called the "women's gospel" is
   a. Matthew.
   b. Mark.
   c. Luke.
   d. John.

6. Jesus sometimes sums up his teachings in
   a. ten commandments.
   b. one commandment.
   c. two commandments.
   d. five commandments.

7. The view that God's imminent divine judgment and the end of the world is near is
   a. messianism.
   b. apocalypticism.
   c. redemption.
   d. schism.

8. Before Paul was converted to belief in Jesus, he was a(n)
   a. Jewish patriot.
   b. Essene.
   c. Sadducee.
   d. Pharisee.

9. Letters written in the New Testament to instruct, encourage, and solve problems are called
   a. Gospels.
   b. Epistles.
   c. Acts.
   d. Revelation.

10. The first major Church council was held in 325 C.E. at
    a. Nicaea.
    b. Jerusalem.
    c. Alexandria.
    d. Chalcedon.

11. The person who essentially shaped over a thousand years of Christianity was
    a. Aquinas.
    b. Benedict.
    c. Francis of Assisi.
    d. Augustine.

12. The event that modernized the Roman Catholic Church was the
    a. Council of Trent.
    b. Counter-Reformation.
    c. Second Vatican Council.
    d. Council of Chalcedon.

13. The Puritans and the Presbyterian Church stand within the tradition of
    a. the Anglican Church.
    b. the Anabaptists.
    c. Luther.
    d. Calvin.

SHORT-ANSWER STUDY QUESTIONS, BY CHAPTER SECTIONS

The Life and Teachings of Jesus

1. Why was Israel so full of unrest at the time of Jesus' birth? (p. 344)

2. What were some of the expectations of those who thought they lived in the "end times"? (p. 344)

3. Describe traditional teachings surrounding the birth of Jesus. (p. 346)

4. Why would Jesus not be well received by the Sadducees and the Jewish patriots? (p. 346)

Jesus in the New Testament Gospels

1. What are the Gospels and how does their viewpoint differ from a historical research report? (p. 346)

2. What were the basic beliefs and practices Jesus embraced as a Jew? (pp. 346–348)

3. Explain Jesus' emphasis on love and its many forms. (p. 348)

4. Describe some other concerns and positions of Jesus. (pp. 348–349)

5. How did Jesus measure up as a social activist? (p. 349)

6. Describe Jesus' views and actions on matters relating to the family. (p. 349)

The Two Great Commandments

1. What are the two Great Commandments that were so important to Jesus? (p. 350)

2. Describe some of the values Jesus had in mind when he used the phrase "Kingdom of God." (p. 350)

3. How might apocalypticism relate to the Kingdom of God in the teachings of Jesus? (p. 350)

Early Christian Beliefs and History

1. Describe the core of the early Christian message. (p. 351)

2. Describe the early Christian group in Jerusalem. (pp. 351–352)

Paul and Pauline Christianity

1. Why is Paul sometimes called the cofounder of Christianity? (p. 352)

2. Discuss Paul's background and the events that led to his support of Jesus. (p. 352)

3. What was Paul's usual missionary technique? (pp. 352–353)

4. Describe Paul's reasoning on his position about whether new converts should keep Jewish laws. (p. 353)

5. What were the ways Paul understood Jesus? (pp. 353–354)

The New Testament: Its Structure and Artistry

1. Briefly describe the four parts of the New Testament and their content. (p. 355)

2. How does the New Testament mirror the structure of the Hebrew Bible? (p. 355)

3. What are the characteristics shared by synoptic gospels? (p. 356)

4. Highlight the features and intended audience of Matthew. (p. 356)

5. Why is the gospel of Mark thought to be the oldest gospel? (p. 356)

6. Characterize the gospel of Luke and its likely intended audience. (pp. 356–357)

7. What features of the gospel of John distinguish it from the synoptics? (pp. 357–358)

8. List some of the symbols used in John to show aspects of Jesus and his meaning for the believer. (p. 358)

9. Why were the Epistles written and what are their general themes? (pp. 358–359)

10. Discuss the characteristics of the Book of Revelation. (p. 359)

The Christian Canon

1. Discuss some of the ways the Christian Bible is read and interpreted by Christians. (p. 360)

2. Why is interpretation of the Christian Bible such a serious and controversial matter? (p. 360)

The Essential Christian Worldview

1. In what ways was the early Christian wordview diverse? (p. 361)

2. How do Christians generally understand God? (p. 361)

3. Discuss the Christian view of Jesus Christ. (p. 361)

4. What are the functions of the Holy Spirit? (p. 363)

5. Explain the Holy Trinity. (p. 363)

6. Describe the Christian view of human life. (p. 363)

7. What are the general views on life after death? (pp. 363–364)

The Early Spread of Christianity

1. What are the stages through which Christianity went in its growth? (p. 364)

2. Describe the basic features of church structure that were adopted. (p. 364)

3. Why is the bishop of Rome known as the pope? (pp. 364–365)

4. What was Constantine's role in the development of Christianity? (pp. 368–369)

5. Offer some examples of Roman influence on Western Christianity. (p. 369)

6. How might some of the Greek and Roman religions have influenced early Christianity? (Box: p. 366)

7. List some of the gods or goddesses and the months and days of the week named after them. (Box: pp. 367–368)

Influences on Christianity at the End of the Roman Empire

Augustine

1. What are some of the details of Augustine's life? (p. 370)

2. How did Augustine influence the development of Christianity? (p. 370)

Benedict and the Monastic Ideal

1. What was the attraction of the monastic way of life? (p. 371)

2. How did the Benedictine order structure the lives of monks? (p. 373)

The Eastern Orthodox Church

Early Development

Describe the origins of the Orthodox branch of Christianity. (p. 374)

Eastern Orthodox Beliefs

1. What questions helped define and differentiate the Orthodox Church? (p. 376)

2. Describe the mystical tendency in the theology of Orthodoxy. (p. 376)

3. Discuss the role of icons. (p. 377)

4. What were some of the factors that led to the first great division within Christianity in 1054? (p. 377)

5. Broadly speaking, how do Western and Eastern Christianity differ? (p. 378)

Christianity in the Middle Ages

What were some of the reasons for the appeal and growth of Christianity? (p. 380)

Christian Mysticism

1. Describe the goals of mysticism in the West. (p. 381)

2. Who were some of the great Christian mystics? (pp. 381–383)

The Crusades, the Inquisition, and the Founding of Religious Orders

1. Why were the Crusades initiated? (p. 383)

2. What was the origin and purpose of the Inquisition? (p. 385)

The Late Middle Ages

What were the reasons for the feeling of pessimism in the Late Middle Ages? (pp. 385–386)

The Protestant Reformation

Why was the Roman Church perhaps in more need of reform than the Eastern Church was? (pp. 386–387)

Martin Luther

Describe Luther's basic position as a Reformer and why he succeeded where others failed. (pp. 387–388)

Forms of Protestantism

1. What are the basic emphases of Protestant Christianity? (Box: p. 389)

2. List the major branches or forms of Protestantism to emerge from the Reformation and some key defining characteristics. (pp. 388–392)

The Development of Christianity Following the Protestant Reformation

The Catholic Reformation (Counter Reformation)

1. Describe the reforms initiated within Catholicism by the Council of Trent. (p. 394)

2. What are the elements stressed within Catholicism, partially as a response to the Protestant Reformation? (Box: p. 394)

The International Spread of Christianity

1. How did Catholicism interact with native religions in the Americas? (p. 395)

2. Describe the role of Protestant churches in the lives of African Americans. (pp. 396–397)

Nontraditional Christianity

1. Briefly relate some of the history and beliefs of the LDS, or Mormon Church. (pp. 397–400)

2. Discuss the origin and beliefs of at least one other of the nontraditional forms of Christianity. (pp. 401–403)

Christian Practice

Sacraments and Other Rituals

1. Discuss the meaning and practice of Baptism. (pp. 403–404)

2. How is the Lord's Supper practiced and what is its significance? (p. 404)

3. List other sacraments accepted by some churches. (pp. 405–406)

4. Describe some devotional rituals, objects, and symbols along with their meaning. (Box: p. 405)

The Christian Year

1. Discuss the focus of Christianity's two most important celebrations. (pp. 406–407)

2. What events are commemorated during Holy Week? (p. 408)

Devotion to Mary

Why do many Christians practice devotion to Mary? (p. 409)

Christianity and the Arts

Architecture

1. Discuss the chief features of either Romanesque or Gothic architecture. (p. 411)

2. How has the Protestant focus influenced church architecture? (p. 412)

Art

Characterize the style and subject matter of icons in Orthodoxy. (pp. 415–416)

Music

Describe some of Christianity's contributions in music. (pp. 417–419)

Christianity Faces the Modern World

The Challenges of Science and Secularism

How has the growth of science and secularism challenged Christianity? (p. 420)

Contemporary Influences and Developments

1. What are the goals in the ecumenical movement? (p. 422)

2. Describe some of the forms of Christian meditation. (Box: p. 423)

3. What changes did Vatican II bring to the Catholic Church? (p. 422)

4. Describe the developments in evangelical denominations. (pp. 423–425)

5. What challenges and changes has feminism brought to Christianity? (p. 425)

POSSIBLE PAPER TOPICS

1. The text makes reference to the impact that biblical scholarship has had on interpretation of the Bible. Research the strategies and techniques of one of the modern approaches, such as form criticism, redaction criticism, or narrative theology.

2. Explore the life of one of the significant missionaries listed in the text. Be sure to research modern appraisals of that person's accomplishments.

3. Many scholars have said that Liberation Theology is the most significant movement in Christianity in the twentieth century. Research the origins and methods of this movement, which led to the deaths of many priests, nuns, and lay leaders throughout Latin America at the hands of military dictators and right-wing death squads.

INTERRELIGIOUS COMPARISONS

1. Some Hindus accept the concept of an avatar, or descent of a God who appears on earth to restore righteousness. Compare this with the Christian understanding of incarnation.

2. Compare and contrast Jesus' use of parables with the purpose and function of koans in Zen Buddhism.

3. Mahayana Buddhism stresses the practice of *karuna*, or compassion for the suffering of all beings. Assess the similarities and differences with the Christian idea of *agape* love.

REFLECTION EXERCISES

1. Many Jews living in the time of Jesus believed they were living in the "end times." And during almost every period of history, some people have believed the same thing. Could we be living in the end time now? How could the end happen? Hollywood has portrayed the end of the world in many ways—nuclear annihilation, invasions, volcanoes and earthquakes, comets or asteroids hitting the earth. Take time to reflect on how you and those around you would react if you knew the end was near. If you can picture this vividly enough, see if it changes some of the things you think are important and valuable.

2. In Paul's understanding of grace in Christianity, one essentially gets a reward or unmerited gift when in fact one deserves exactly the opposite. Think of times when you "had it coming" for something you had done that was clearly wrong. Have there been times when the party wronged actually forgave you? What impact did it have on you? And what about the reverse situation? Feeling hurt and anger, somehow you were able to let go of the feelings and forgive instead of seeking "paybacks." Was it easy or hard? What finally did or did not enable you to forgive?

3. Jesus advocated nonviolence and not judging others. Some say you can do this only if you expect the end of the world tomorrow! Is it possible? What's the value? Don't you have to make so many exceptions and qualifications to the rule that soon it has no real content? What do you think?

4. One of the things that Jesus urged was simplicity, recommending that people become like little children (Matt. 18:3). Elsewhere Paul talked about putting childish ways behind him and growing up (1 Cor. 13). What gives? Is this one of those glaring contradictions that would-be debunkers of the Bible like to point out? How do you resolve this? In what ways should we be like children and and in what ways like adults?

ANSWERS

Fill In the Blank

1. orthodox
2. apostle
3. eucharist
4. dogma
5. icon
6. incarnation
7. sin
8. redemption or atonement
9. gospel
10. Predestination

Multiple Choice

1. d
2. b
3. a
4. d
5. c
6. c
7. b
8. d
9. b
10. a
11. d
12. c
13. d

CHAPTER 10

ISLAM

LEARNING OBJECTIVES

After reading this chapter, you should be able to

♦ describe Muhammad's life and the major events that shaped Islam.

♦ describe the Muslim view of God.

♦ describe the Five Pillars of Islam.

♦ discuss the significance and content of the Qu'ran for Muslims.

♦ explain the differences between the Sunni and Shiite branches of Islam.

♦ describe the belief and practices of Islam's mystics.

♦ discuss Islam's influence on the arts.

CHAPTER SUMMARY

In a cave near Mecca, amid the mountains and deserts of Arabia, a caravan driver sought religious truth in his solitary meditations. When he was 40, a bright presence came to him in his first revelation. Shaken and questioning his experience, but with encouragement from his wife, Muhammad became convinced that he had experienced a true communication from God. More revelations followed over a period of approximately twenty years. They became the Qu'ran, believed by Muslims to be the purest revelation from God.

From a persecuted prophet with a small following, Muhammad became a successful military and political leader. He extended Islam over his former opponents in Mecca and then throughout Arabia. After his death, Islam continued to spread rapidly. Within a hundred years, the Muslims ruled an area between two and three times the size of the Roman Empire.

Muhammad proclaimed a surrender or submission to the one powerful and transcendent God who was also worshiped by the Jews and the Christians. These two religions received the true revelation but had contaminated or misunderstood it in various ways. He therefore saw himself as the last of a long line of prophets, clarifying God's will in a definitive and final way.

Islam stresses the power of a God who controls every detail of life. Religion is viewed as a strongly ethical enterprise and provides patterns for ideal living, on both the personal and the sociopolitical level. The Five Pillars of Islam define core religious practices. A simple and straightforward creed proclaims one God, with Muhammad as his messenger. Prayer is to be performed at five prescribed times a day, facing in the direction of Mecca. Charity to the poor is the third pillar that helps create a compassionate heart in the believer and a more just society. Fasting during the month of Ramadan is the fourth pillar, and pilgrimage to Mecca at least once during one's life is the fifth.

A dispute over Muhammad's successor led to the split between the Sunni and Shiite branches of Islam. The Sunnis comprise nearly eighty-five percent of all Muslims and ruled over the Muslim world during its golden age, which spanned nearly five hundred years. This golden age saw significant developments in law, science, philosophy, and the arts. The Shiites believe that the true hereditary successors of Muhammad possessed a special spiritual power. Most suffered a martyr's death at the hands of the Sunni usurpers.

The Sufis embody Islam's mystical element. They emerged as a reaction to the wealth, luxury, and excesses surrounding the powerful caliphate and sought a return to simplicity. Often in conflict with religious authorities, Sufis seek a direct experience of God in this life. Sufi missionaries helped in the spread of Islam, and Sufi poets created some of the world's greatest poetry.

Islamic architecture produced the great mosques with their tall towers and huge domes. They convey a sense of simplicity and grandeur, of harmony and balance that echo the values and convictions of Islam. Islamic art has combined elements of both the austere and the ornate, from prayer rugs and gardens inspired by images of paradise to elegantly written and chanted verses of the Qu'ran.

Islamic civilization began to eclipse nearly 500 years ago by the West, but has experienced resurgence in more recent times. Islam continues to gain converts and has also spread through emigration. Traditional Islam is grappling with challenges from secularism, new styles of government and commerce, the roles of women and men, and the onslaught of Western popular culture. Highly varied responses are being attempted by different Muslim societies. Dissimilar values and social ideals have led to conflicts between Islamic and Western cultures that shape many geo-political issues today.

FILL IN THE BLANK

1. The pilgrimage every Muslim should make to _____ (city) is called the _____ (Arabic word).

2. A muslim place of worship is a _____.

3. Submission to God is the central meaning of _____.

4. _____ represents the devotional movements and mystical elements of Islam.

5. God's words as revealed to Muhammad are found in the _____.

6. An _____ is a religious leader, specifically one venerated in Shiite Islam that is a hereditary successor of Muhammad.

7. Muhammad's flight from Mecca to Medina is the _____.

8. _____ literally means "struggle" and refers to the ideal of spreading Islamic belief and practice.

9. The month of fasting is _____.

10. A chapter in Islam's holy book is called a _____.

MULTIPLE CHOICE

1. The Sunni and Shiite branches of Islam split over a dispute about
   a. whether or not to have a lunar calendar.
   b. how many wives were acceptable.
   c. succession after Muhammad.
   d. when the pilgrimage should be performed.

2. The Muslim calendar began on
   a. Muhammad's birthday.
   b. Muhammad's flight to Yathrib.
   c. the night Muhammad received his revelation.
   d. the date of Muhammad's death.

3. The caliph was
   a. a religious and political leader.
   b. head of the mystical branch of Islam.
   c. the name given to an opponent of Muhammad.
   d. the magic horse Muhammad rode on his ascent to heaven.

4. The holy object within the square shrine of the Kabah is
   a. a black meteorite.
   b. a nail from the cross of Jesus.
   c. the tomb of Muhammad.
   d. the first Qu'ran.

5. The word Allah means
   a. the Merciful.
   b. the Just.
   c. the Compassionate.
   d. the God.

6. The Qu'ran speaks of the following religious figure(s):
   a. Jesus.
   b. Buddha.
   c. St. Paul.
   d. all of the above.

7. The Taj Mahal is located in
   a. Spain.
   b. Turkey.
   c. Iran.
   d. India.

8. The branch of Islam that believes the successor to Muhammad should have been a male directly descended from the prophet's immediate family is called
   a. Sunni.
   b. Shiite.
   c. Sufi.
   d. Hasidic.

9. In addition to basing rules for daily life on the Qu'ran, Muslims appeal to the hadith, the
   a. laws of nature.
   b. rulings of the successors to Muhammad.
   c. the sayings of Khadijah, Muhammad's wife.
   d. recollections people had of Muhammad's words and actions.

10. Muslims believe in
   a. resurrection of the body.
   b. a final judgment.
   c. neither a nor b.
   d. both a and b.

11. Muhammad's job before he became a prophet was a
   a. merchant.
   b. date grower.
   c. caravan driver.
   d. camel breeder.

12. A religious requirement for male Muslims, also necessary for male Jews, is
   a. circumcision.
   b. drinking wine on special feast days.
   c. wearing of the turban.
   d. marriage.

13. Along with Judaism, Islam forbids
   a. eating unleavened bread.
   b. wearing of the veil by women.
   c. eating pork.
   d. wearing gold jewelry.

SHORT-ANSWER STUDY QUESTIONS, BY CHAPTER SECTIONS

The Life and Teachings of Muhammad

1. Offer a short biography of Muhammad. (pp. 432–435)

2. Characterize the situation in and around Arabia during Muhammad's time. (pp. 434–435)

3. Muhammad's religious views were not well received at first. Why? (p. 435)

4. What purpose did Muhammad's Night Journey, or Ascent to Heaven, serve in his life? (p. 435)

5. Describe how Muhammad is viewed by Muslims today. (p. 437)

Essentials of Islam

1. How is God viewed and described in Islam? (pp. 437–439)

2. How does Islam view its relationship with Christianity and Judaism? (pp. 437–439)

3. What is the role and function of prophets according to Islam? (p. 439)

4. Discuss the significance of Abraham for Muslims, Jews, and Christians. (pp. 439–440)

The Five Pillars of Islam

1. Briefly describe each of the Five Pillars. (pp. 440–445)

2. Trace the theme of simplicity in Islam, for example, in its creed, death rituals, dress during the Hajj, appeal in Sufism, and architecture. (pp. 442–444)

3. What purposes does fasting serve in Islam? (pp. 442–443)

4. Highlight the main features of the Hajj and its overall impact on believers. (pp. 443–444)

Additional Islamic Religious Practices

1. Summarize additional Islamic religious practices, and state how Muslims view all the controls and prohibitions. (pp. 446–448)

2. Discuss the condition of women in pre-Islamic Arab culture and the reforms Muhammad made. (Box: p. 448)

3. Explore the current trends on the role of women in the Muslim world. (Box: pp. 448–449)

Scripture: The Qur'an

Describe the content of the Qur'an and its role in shaping Islamic life. (pp. 449–452)

The Historical Development of Islam

Expansion and Consolidation

1. Trace the rapid spread of Islam on a map or globe of the world. What elements within and without Islam contributed to the rapid spread? (pp. 452–453)

2. Date the golden age of Islam and describe its contributions and achievements. (p. 454)

The Shiite and Sunni Division within Islam

1. Discuss the origin of the Sunni-Shiite split in Islam. (pp. 454–455)

2. Describe the main features of Shiite Islam, especially regarding the role of *imams*. What has generated the most divisions within Shiite Islam? (pp. 455–456)

3. What are the general features of Sunni Islam? (pp. 456–457)

4. Discuss some of the major movements within Sunni Islam. (pp. 457–458)

Sufism: Islamic Mysticism

Describe the origins of Sufism and its attraction for many Muslims. (p. 459)

Sufi Beliefs

1. What are the goals of Sufi mysticism? (pp. 459–460)

2. Why has Sufism often been controversial or come into conflict with the religious authorities? (pp. 460–461)

Sufi Practice and Poetry

Give an example of a Sufi interpretation of the Qu'ran or of poetry that is symbolic or allegorical. (pp. 462–463)

Islamic Law and Philosophy

What resources have Muslims used to address the many aspects of human life? (p. 466)

Islamic Law and Legal Institutions

1. What is a theocratic state? How is it justified in the Muslim view? (p. 467)

2. Discuss the meanings of *jihad*. (p. 467)

Islamic Philosophy and Theology

1. Describe some of the philosophic questions explored in Islamic philosophy. How do they compare to the philosophic questions explored in the chapter on Christianity? (p. 468)

2. Define the two philosophic poles within Islam. If you were a Muslim, which would be more appealing to you and why? (pp. 468–469)

Islam and the Arts

Architecture

1. Distinguish the key features of a mosque and how they relate to Muslim religious practice. (p. 470)

2. How do towers and domes relate with the concept of negative space? (p. 471)

Fine Art

1. How are the themes of Paradise expressed in Muslim art? (p. 474)

2. What are the two means of experiencing the Qu'ran, each with its own special beauty? (pp. 474–475)

Islam and the Modern World

Islam and Contemporary Life

1. Describe the challenges modern life presents to traditional Islam. (p. 477)

2. Define secularism and its various political and religious implications. (p. 477)

3. Situate the following countries on a spectrum from adopting Western values to resisting them, explaining why you place them where you do: Turkey, Saudi Arabia, Iran, Egypt. What would be the key arguments offered by both ends of the spectrum—secular state vs. a theocratic Islamist state? (pp. 478–479)

4. Review elements of conflict in at least two other countries with large Muslim populations. (pp. 479–480)

Islam in the West and Beyond

1. What has been the attraction of Islam for converts? (p. 481)

2. What are the origins and appeal of the Nation of Islam in the United States? (p. 481)

3. Describe the strong differences between Islam and mainstream European and American cultures? (p. 483)

4. Discuss the role of the Palestinian issue—attacks and bombings in the West, the legacy of colonialism, and popular culture—in conflicts and clashes between the Muslim world and the West. (pp. 483–484)

5. What lessons from history provide hope that Islamic and Western cultures might successfully change and coexist peacefully? (p. 485)

POSSIBLE PAPER TOPICS

1. Explore the history and cultural features of one of the secondary centers of Islam, such as Córdoba, Granada, or Delhi, that were sometimes totally independent caliphates.

2. Examine the life and thought of one of the Sufis, such as Rabia or Rumi, or one of the great poets—Omar Khayyam, Hafiz, Jami.

3. Research the strategies that one or more Islamic societies or countries are employing to meet the challenges of modernity.

4. Assume you work for a firm in the eastern world and your CEO has asked you to write up a plan for opening a branch office in a Muslim country in the Near East. Its employees would include people from your country and the local labor force. What adaptations would be required to increase the likelihood of success? What measures would you advise to minimize intercultural conflict? (Thanks to Fr. Joseph Hirsch of Regis University for this topic.)

INTERRELIGIOUS COMPARISONS

1. Compare the use and meaning of empty space in Islamic architecture with that in Taoist-inspired drawings.

2. Compare and contrast passages in a translation of the Qu'ran that seem to cast women in a submissive role to passages in the New Testament (1 Corinthians 14:34–35; Ephesians 5:21–27; 1 Timothy 2:11–14). Research various interpretations of each.

3. Explore specific marriage practices and rituals in Islam and compare with those of Hinduism or Judaism. Recognize that great variety exists between countries or regions within the same religion.

REFLECTION EXERCISES

1. Our society is often characterized by its quest for newness and change. This is seen in the latest trends in fashions, home furnishings, automotive design, and what is popular in music. Magazines feature lists of "what's in, what's out, what's hot, what's not." Contrast this with some fundamental features of Islamic culture—the repetition of daily prayer, the frequent hearing of the words of the Qu'ran, and how the repetition of phrases and images is comforting to hearers. What in your own life is repetitious yet is meaningful and brings comfort? Reflect on ways you might enhance this aspect of your life.

2. Many Muslims have traditionally used prayer rugs on which to perform their daily worship and praise. These have served the functional purpose of protecting one's clothes in whatever environment the worshiper finds himself when the call to prayer occurs. Yet on a symbolic level, a sacred space is created that is oriented to Mecca and connects the worshiper to all it represents. The design on the carpets often reflects concepts of Paradise with flowers and fountains, or it often has an image of the Kabah, which is the centerpiece of the Hajj. Perhaps like the flying carpets of Arabian lore, they metaphorically transport the rider—this time to a spiritual place or state evoked by the images.

   If you were a Muslim, what would your ideal prayer rug look like? Perhaps leaving the religion of Islam behind, develop and draw a design for a prayer rug that reflects your own spirituality. What images would be on it? In what direction would you point it? Try making one on paper or drawing it on cloth (approx. 26" by 44"), and explore your thoughts and feelings while using it.

3. During the Hajj, one Muslim said she had never been crowded in such a large throng of people as when circling the Kabah, yet never felt so alone and close to Allah. Have you ever been in an extremely large crowd united in purpose? What was the experience like? How might it be similar and different from the Hajj? You might interview someone who went to the Million-Man March or who has participated in a Promise Keepers Rally. Analyze their experiences and develop into a paper.

4. It has been said that quite a few Arabs who initially opposed Muhammad's message were so overwhelmed by the Qu'ran's beauty when they first heard it recited that they instantly converted. Can you image such an impact of beauty in your own life? What would it be?

5. If you were asked by the CEO of a United States company to set up a branch office in an Islamic country, staffed by both locals and Americans, what considerations and adaptations would be required? This could become a full-fledged project for business majors. Since there are 43 primarily Islamic nation-states, the project could involve researching the unique features of one of them. (Thanks to Fr. Joseph Hirsch of Regis University for this idea.)

ANSWERS

Fill In the Blank

1. Mecca, Hajj
2. mosque
3. Islam
4. Sufism
5. Qur'an
6. imam
7. hijra
8. Jihad
9. Ramadan
10. Sura

Multiple Choice

1. c
2. b
3. a
4. a
5. d
6. a
7. d
8. b
9. d
10. d
11. c
12. a
13. c

CHAPTER 11

ALTERNATIVE PATHS

LEARNING OBJECTIVES

After reading this chapter, you should be able to

♦ describe the factors that help generate new religious movements.

♦ discuss the reasons why new religious movements are controversial or often viewed with suspicion.

♦ summarize the possible relationships between new religions and established religions.

♦ discuss specific new religions that share features with indigenous religions.

♦ discuss specific new religions that incorporate elements of Hinduism, Buddhism, or Chinese religions.

♦ discuss specific new religions with strong Christian or Islamic roots.

♦ clarify the general features that attract followers to many new religions.

CHAPTER SUMMARY

Religions change, grow, and sometimes emerge in response to immigration, social problems, controversies within existing religions, or through individuals having unique experiences. A new religion may start as a variant of established religion that grows into an independent form. It may be syncretic—a blend of different existing religions. Finally, a new religion may surface independent and distinct of established religions.

New religions are often viewed with suspicion. While some new movements may pose a danger to society, most do not. Indeed, many of the major established religions began under similar circumstances and were small, sometimes persecuted movements.

Sharing features with indigenous religions are Contemporary Paganism and Yoruba-tradition religions. Contemporary Pagan movements attempt to return to earlier, nature-based religions that predate Christianity. The movement of Wicca focuses on the feminine aspect of the divine, the prominent role of women as leaders, and seasonal ritual ceremonies. The Druid movement seeks to reclaim the religion of the ancient Celts and focuses on the male aspect of the divine. The religions of Santería, Voodoo, and Candomblé arose among slaves brought to the New World. These syncretic religions blend West African Yoruba traditions and Roman Catholicism. Practitioners believe in a single High God, supernatural beings who mediate between God and humans, and spirits of the dead that can affect the living.

Theosophy and Scientology draw on the traditions of Hinduism and Buddhism. Theosophists speak of multiple spiritual levels and psychic abilities that can be developed through training and meditation. Theosophy and its offshoots helped popularize in the West elements such as reincarnation, karma, and yoga. Scientology was founded in the 1950s by author L. Ron Hubbard. Scientology seeks to correct the process of knowing and interacting with the world to free the soul in progressive stages. This religion acknowledges past lives and has developed its own unique terminology describing the practices that overcome difficulties and blockages in life.

Falun Gong is a new religion much persecuted in present-day China whose roots lie in Taoism and Chinese Buddhism. Followers practice Qigong exercises composed of movement meditations with the goals of gaining health, strength, virtues, and paranormal powers. Another strongly Chinese religion is Cao Dai, which blends elements of Taoism, Confucianism, Buddhism, Chinese belief in spirits, and Christian monotheism.

The Rastafarian movement arose in Jamaica in the 1930s and is strongly influenced by Christianity. Themes of social justice and freedom from oppression run strong in this religion that found a messianic figure in the Ethiopian Emperor Haile Selassie, believed to be a new appearance of Jesus.

Baha'i is a monotheistic religion with roots in Shiite Islam claiming the most advanced revelations from God. Teachings seek ways of harmonizing different religions with each other and with science. Baha'is advocate complete equality between men and women, an end to poverty and racial prejudice, and education for all.

New religious movements offer adherents a unique identity and sense of purpose in the context of small-group intimacy. Women play a key role in many of the new movements. The mystical element often is stressed as followers seek experiences beyond the normal and mundane. Many paths also offer clear programs for self-development.

FILL IN THE BLANK

1. New religious movements that are a blend of different religions are called _____.

2. _____ is a general name for religious movements attempting to return to earlier, nature-based religions.

3. Wiccan seasonal turning points are called _____.

4. In Santería, any deity is called an _____.

5. In Scientology, the _____ is the name for the human soul.

6. Another name for the Emperor Haile Selassie of Ethiopia is _____.

7. Baha'u'llah is the founder of _____.

8. The religion blending Confucianism, Taoism, Buddhism, and Catholic Christianity is _____.

9. Madame Blavatsky is the founder of _____.

10. The _____ movement began in the eighteenth century as an attempt to re-introduce the religion practiced in France and England by the Celts about 2000 years ago.

MULTIPLE CHOICE

1. The midwinter solstice celebration of Wicca is most commonly called the
   a. Samhain.
   b. Beltane.
   c. Yule.
   d. Esbat.

2. Established groups of Wiccans are called
   a. witches.
   b. sisterhoods.
   c. covens.
   d. sects.

3. The word "Voodoo" comes from the Fon word "vodun," whose meaning is
   a. saint way.
   b. oak-tree wisdom.
   c. moon worship.
   d. mysterious power.

4. The youngest alternative path studied in this chapter is
   a. Falun Gong.
   b. Rastafarian.
   c. Cao Dai.
   d. Scientology.

5. In practicing their religion, both Baha'is and Muslims
   a. engage in periods of fasting and undertake pilgrimages.
   b. observe a lunar calendar and abstain from drinking alcohol.
   c. abstain from alcohol and engage in periods of fasting.
   d. meet in nine-sided mosques or temples.

6. Two new religions that blend aspects of Christianity into their beliefs and practices are
   a. Wicca and Voodoo.
   b. Cao Dai and Santería.
   c. Rastafarianism and Falun Gong.
   d. Rastafarianism and Scientology.

7. The biggest influence of Rastafarianism on mainstream culture has been
   a. reggae music.
   b. organic and natural food diet.
   c. dreadlocks.
   d. distinctive dress with four symbolic colors.

8. Worship and celebration of the feminine aspect of the divine is practiced most by the
   a. Druids.
   b. Baha'is.
   c. Rastafarians.
   d. Wiccans.

9. The Baha'is found a messianic figure in
   a. a young Persian aristocrat.
   b. an Ethiopian king.
   c. a writer of science fiction.
   d. a Jamaican farmer.

10. The "world teacher" prophesied by Madame Blavatsky was later identified as
    a. Elizabeth Claire Prophet.
    b. Rudolf Steiner.
    c. L. Ron Hubbard.
    d. J. Krishnamurti.

11. Working with an "auditor" to find and remove areas that have created blockages to personal growth is a practice of
    a. Scientology.
    b. Theosophy.
    c. Church Universal and Triumphant.
    d. Voodoo.

12. The religions of the Yoruba tradition and Rastafarianism have significant connections with
    a. the Middle East.
    b. India.
    c. Africa.
    d. China.

13. The breath and visualization exercises of Qigong that circulate energy through the body are further enhanced in Falun Gong when a master
    a. ritually eliminates bad karma of the disciple.
    b. activates an invisible spiritual wheel in the lower abdomen of the disciple.
    c. projects the image of a large eye inside a triangle into the disciple's mind.
    d. trains the disciple to be "mounted" by beings from a higher realm.

SHORT-ANSWER STUDY QUESTIONS, BY CHAPTER SECTIONS

Origins of New Religions

1. What are some of the forces prompting change in religions? (p. 490)

2. List the possible developmental relationships between new religious movements and established traditions. (pp. 490–491)

"Cults," "Sects," and New Religious Movements

1. Why do new religious movements often generate suspicion and tension with larger and older religions? (Box: p. 491)

2. Define "sect" and "cult" in both academic and popular meanings. (Box: p. 491)

3. Why should some new religious movements be viewed with caution while others with tolerance? (Box: p. 491)

Contemporary Paganism: Wicca and Druidism

1. What are some of the possible reasons that movements reclaiming ancient nature-based religions attract followers? (p. 492)

2. Discuss the various meanings of the word *pagan*. (pp. 492–493)

3. Describe the essentials shared by the different strands of Wicca. (p. 493)

4. What is the general seasonal structure of Wiccan religious practice? (p. 493)

5. Explain the two core ethical principles of Wicca. (pp. 493–494)

6. What are the arguments for and against Wicca being an ancient religion? (p. 494)

7. Who were the ancient Druids? (p. 496)

8. What features does the modern Druidic movement share with Wicca? (p. 497)

Religions of the Yoruba Tradition: Santería, Voodoo, and Candomblé

1. Discuss the roots of these three religions and why they are practiced in the Western Hemisphere. (p. 497)

2. Explain the difference between syncretism and Raul Canizares' term *dissimulation*. (pp. 498–499)

3. Describe the similarities between Roman Catholicism and Yoruba religion that may have encouraged syncretism. (pp. 499–500)

4. How is the Yoruba High God different from that of Roman Catholicism? (p. 500)

5. What are the parallels between the gods of the Greeks and Romans and the *orishas* of Yoruba religion? (p. 500)

6. Describe typical aspects of services in the Yoruba traditions. (p. 500)

Theosophy

1. Name the sources Madame Blavatsky used to form Theosophy. (p. 501)

2. Describe the view of reality generally shared by all Theosophists. (p. 502)

3. Explain the relationship J. Krishnamurti had with Theosophy. (p. 502)

4. List some of the offshoots of Theosophy and their special concerns. (pp. 502–503)

5. Discuss the influence of Madame Blavatsky and Theosophy on other movements. (p. 503)

Scientology

1. Describe the various ways the goal of Scientology is stated. (p. 504)

2. Summarize the parallels between Scientology and Hinduism. (p. 504)

3. What does "The Bridge" describe? (p. 504)

4. Describe in general terms how one becomes "clear" through processing. (p. 504)

Falun Gong

1. What strands of traditional Chinese religious practice are utilized in Falun Gong? (p. 504)

2. What benefits do followers of Falun Gong seek? (pp. 505–506)

3. Why might the Chinese government be attempting to suppress this movement? (p. 506)

Cao Dai

1. How did this religion begin? (pp. 506–507)

2. Describe the three great phases of revelation called "Alliances." (p. 507)

3. What symbolism might one see in a Cao Dai church? (p. 507)

4. Describe the influences of Christianity, Buddhism, and Confucianism on Cao Dai. (p. 507)

Rastafarianism

1. What role did Jamaica's colonial past play in shaping this religion? (p. 509)

2. Describe Marcus Garvey's contributions to Rastafarianism. (p. 509)

3. Discuss the status of native Ethiopian king Ras Tafari for believers. (p. 509)

4. List the four shared beliefs held by the different branches of this religion. (pp. 510–511)

5. What representative practices have developed in the Rastafarian movement? (pp. 511–512)

Baha'i

1. Describe the features of Shiite Islam that are significant to the emergence of Baha'i. (p. 513)

2. Explain the Baha'i understanding of other religions. (p. 514)

3. What does Baha'i teach about the afterlife? (p. 514)

4. Summarize ways Baha'i would improve human life in this world. (p. 514)

5. Why do Baha'is advocate an auxiliary world language and a single world government? (pp. 514–515)

6. List some of the religious practices or behaviors endorsed by the Baha'i religion. (p. 515)

New Religious Movements: A Special Role

1. List the four elements of many new religious movements that are attractive to people. (p. 516)

POSSIBLE PAPER TOPICS

1. Investigate the elements causing some new religious movements to become a danger to either society or their followers.

2. Explore the life of a key figure in one of the new religious movements like Marcus Garvey, L. Ron Hubbard, or J. Krishnamurti.

3. Examine the effect of religious persecution on one of the new religious movements.

INTERRELIGIOUS COMPARISONS

1. Explore the similarities between Christianity and Baha'i in origins and teachings.

2. Further research the similarities and differences between the two Contemporary Pagan religions of Wicca and the Druid movement.

3. Discuss the similarities and differences between the sacramental use of marijuana in Rastafarianism and wine in Christian communion or peyote in the Native American Church.

REFLECTION EXERCISES

1. Try your hand at creating a new religion. Reviewing the patterns and elements of religion explored in Chapter 1 of the text could be a good place to start. A more right-brained approach might begin with a vision of the believers gathering together. How are they dressed? What symbols are displayed? What rituals are practiced? Then you can start explaining the meanings, origins, and doctrines. Finally, assess your new religion from the perspective of this chapter. Is it a new offshoot of an existing religion or is it syncretic? Does your new religion manifest the elements summarized at the end of the chapter that people find attractive in NRMs?

2. Research the origins of a major established religion or denomination. Imaginatively place yourself in the time it first emerged. Visualize the setting and the people involved. What were the major issues and controversies? What would your role have been? Experience the conflicting thoughts, the feelings, and the excitement of being present as this religion first took form.

ANSWERS

Fill In the Blank

1. syncretic
2. Contemporary Pagan
3. Sabbats
4. Ocha
5. thetan
6. Ras Tafari
7. Baha'i
8. Cao Dai
9. Theosophy
10. Druid

Multiple Choice

1. c
2. c
3. d
4. a
5. c
6. b
7. a
8. d
9. a
10. d
11. a
12. c
13. b

CHAPTER 12

THE MODERN SEARCH

LEARNING OBJECTIVES

After reading this chapter, you should be able to

♦ describe profound changes in the modern world.

♦ discuss the impact of the women's movement, science, and secularism.

♦ explain the process of religious change and accommodation.

♦ discuss the phenomenon of fundamentalism.

♦ discuss the place nature has in religious thought.

♦ explain the features of eclectic spirituality.

CHAPTER SUMMARY

Religions by nature seem to be conservative. Yet the modern world has endured profound changes in economics, politics, lifestyles, and cultural interactions. It really is virtually impossible for separate religions to remain separate any longer. Some of the greatest challenges facing religion in the modern world come from three areas—the women's movement, science, and secularism. The women's rights movement is striving to eliminate traditional restrictions placed on women. This has led to a greater role for women in religious leadership and sensitivity to the use of inclusive language. Also there has been a renewed religious appreciation of feminine concerns and even an exploration of feminine aspects of the divine in some groups. A parallel development is the reassessment of the role and purpose of sexuality in human life. This has led to the questioning of traditional sexual ethics and prohibitions in religious traditions.

Controversies and sometimes contradictory stances have been developed by religions around such issues as divorce, birth control, use of violence, and same-gender relationships. Many modern changes are driven by science and technology. Scientific theories have transformed our view of the universe, from Big Bang cosmology to Darwinian evolution. On a more basic level, we now know causes of illness and natural disasters, yet these are still sometimes called "acts of God," which reflects an earlier prescientific view. Industrialization and technology have produced environmental degradation but also reduced mortality rates, increased standards of living, and extended life spans. The growth of secularism, or the separation of religion from everyday life, is another change that challenges traditional religions. Also, more people today admit to atheism or agnosticism without fear of scorn.

Yet the religious impulse is alive and well despite the above challenges. Spiritual themes and images permeate popular culture in films, music, and television. Even the news media regularly includes reports on religion. In spite of historical and contemporary clashes, representatives of different religions increasingly meet to discuss their similarities and differences and to focus on common concerns.

All religions that survive somehow adapt to changing circumstances whether they acknowledge the adaptations or not. The process is a painful struggle in which the pendulum swings back and forth between retrenchment and radical change. The conservative reaction to the massive changes of the modern world can be seen in fundamentalistic movements, which share similar features in widely divergent religions.

At the opposite end of the spectrum is a turn to nature as a spiritual path. Another development in the modern world is the appearance of an eclectic spirituality that attempts to assemble elements of different belief systems to satisfy needs met traditionally by one religion. Though difficult to define because of its diversity, modern spirituality generally manifests three aspects or values: interrelatedness of all reality, reverence and respect of others and nature that is capable of seeing the miraculous in the ordinary, and a contemplative stance that seeks experiences of inner peace and a feeling of harmony between oneself and the outer world.

FILL IN THE BLANK

1. The term for easy access to other cultures that may lead to a kind of unification of culture is _____.

2. Recognizing and affirming the value of different cultures is called _____.

3. Religious values of poverty, simplicity, and detachment have been challenged by _____.

4. Worldwide interconnections challenge a narrow, provincial focus that is also known as _____.

5. The term _____ refers to the modern tendency to separate religion from everyday life.

6. The term for the position that the existence of God can neither be proved nor disproved is _____.

7. Concern for nature and its preservation is called _____.

8. _____ is partially explained by the conservative religious reaction to the onslaught of change.

9. The new type of environmentally sensitive travel to visit natural preserves and experience other wonders of nature is called _____.

10. The term the author uses to describe the whole movement that finds great spiritual significance in the environment is _____.

MULTIPLE CHOICE

1. Earth Day is celebrated each year on
   a. March 21.
   b. April 15.
   c. April 22.
   d. May 5.

2. The greatest impetus to separate religion from public life in Western history came from
   a. interactions with other cultures and religions.
   b. religious leaders reflecting on the principles of their tradition.
   c. atheistic philosophies that gained popularity.
   d. religious wars between different Christian groups in the sixteenth and seventeenth centuries.

3. Translations of sacred literature and prayers that attempt to be more gender-neutral are
   a. one result of the women's rights movement.
   b. a product of fundamentalist concerns.
   c. an attempt to reestablish patriarchal religion.
   d. generated by interfaith dialogue.

4. Considering sexuality, the world's religions generally
   a. are silent on the subject.
   b. accept it for procreation only.
   c. prize virginity and celibacy.
   d. express a great variety of attitudes.

5. Science that leads to specific inventions or other practical benefits is called
   a. theoretical science.
   b. abstract science.
   c. applied science.
   d. agnostic science.

6. According to the author, religions in the future will continue to be challenged by the secular vision particularly when
   a. they engage in missionary efforts.
   b. they have to work in secular political situations.
   c. dealing with new moral issues.
   d. engaging in interfaith dialogue.

7. Because Marxist Communism took on many of religion's attributes, many scholars think that it
   a. is an example of a nontheistic religion.
   b. betrayed its atheistic ideology.
   c. secretly advocated belief in God.
   d. really was capitalistic.

8. Roman Catholicism's Second Vatican Council is an example of
   a. separation of church and state.
   b. accommodation to ancient church doctrines.
   c. fundamentalism.
   d. accommodation to modern scientific and cultural changes.

9. Something that has become a significant modern religious icon expressing interconnection is
   a. the image of two hands together.
   b. the Internet.
   c. the photo of earth taken from the moon.
   d. the rock concert.

10. Because of a modern reappraisal of the value and worth of nature,
    a. technology has challenged religion.
    b. oral religions are being looked to with new respect.
    c. human beings are attempting to control the power of nature.
    d. secular ideas have gained ground.

11. The Naturism movement lacks only a strong parallel with the
    a. sacramental and ritualistic element.
    b. prophetic aspect.
    c. mystical aspect.
    d. secular element.

12. Many of the role models associated with Naturism are
    a. religious leaders from the West.
    b. religious leaders from the East.
    c. ancient figures.
    d. women.

13. Aspects of Buddhism, modern cosmology, quantum physics, and the paintings of Georgia O'Keeffe have been used to demonstrate
    a. respect and reverence.
    b. abstraction.
    c. interrelatedness.
    d. the contemplative stance.

SHORT-ANSWER STUDY QUESTIONS, BY CHAPTER SECTIONS

Modern Influences on the Future of Religion

The New World Order

1. Describe how the social, political, and economic landscape has changed to produce the new world order. (p. 525)

2. Discuss the effect modern capitalism has had on the world and on religion. (pp. 525–526)

3. Define globalism and urbanism and explain their challenge to traditional religion. (p. 526)

Multiculturalism and Interfaith Dialogue

1. What factors have made contact across different cultures practically unavoidable? (pp. 526–527)

2. Discuss some of the ways different traditions have adapted to changes in the world. (p. 527)

3. What are some points of contact or common ground that have served as a basis for interfaith dialogues? (p. 527)

Women's Rights Movements

1. How have women been restricted in many societies? (p. 528)

2. What developments have begun to affect attitudes regarding the roles of women? (pp. 529–530)

3. Give examples of some religious groups that have opened leadership roles to women. (p. 530)

4. List a few religious groups that have resisted allowing women leadership positions. (p. 529)

5. Describe ways that the women's movement has already affected religious practices. (p. 530)

Reassessment of Human Sexuality

1. What factors have prompted a reexamination of human sexuality? (pp. 530–531)

2. Contrast traditional views of the purpose of sex with other functions it serves. (p. 531)

3. Describe some of the areas of debate and controversy in religion surrounding marriage and sex. (pp. 531–532)

Science and Technology

1. Briefly summarize the current scientific view of reality. (pp. 533–534)

2. What are some of the new choices and ethical questions given to us by science and technology? (pp. 535–537)

3. What have been the benefits and liabilities of the scientific approach to reality? (p. 537)

Secularism

1. What is secularism? (p. 538)

2. How does agnosticism relate with a secular view? (pp. 538–539)

3. In what ways did Communism manifest religious attributes? (p. 539)

4. Summarize the sometimes conflicting views on violence in the religious texts and traditions of Jainism, Buddhism, Hinduism, Taoism, Judaism, Christianity, and Islam. (Box: pp. 540–541)

Environmental Challenges

What are some of the threats to the environment that have raised new moral questions? (pp. 540–543)

The Recurring Challenge of Change

1. What are the two possible common denominators existing in every religion? (p. 543)

2. In what major ways has the Roman Catholic church adapted to modern changes? (pp. 543–544)

3. Define the phenomenon of fundamentalism. (p. 544)

4. Give some examples of twentieth-century fundamentalism. (pp. 544–545)

Naturism: A New Religious Phenomenon?

1. Discuss how human beings have tried to control or minimize the power of nature. (p. 545)

2. How has nature been negatively viewed by some religions? (p. 546)

3. What are some of the reasons nature is being viewed differently today? (p. 546)

4. What religions have traditionally esteemed nature? (p. 546)

5. How has an appreciation of nature been expressed recently in the West? (p. 547)

6.   What are the religious parallels appearing in Naturism? (pp. 547–549)

Eclectic Spirituality

Describe the particular set of attitudes and practices associated with eclectic spirituality. (p. 550)

Religion and Movies

What spiritual concerns have been addressed in films? (Box: p. 551)

Interrelatedness

Discuss the feature of interrelatedness in eclectic spirituality. (p. 553)

Religion and Pop Culture

Describe aspects of popular culture that present religious themes. (Box: p. 553)

Reverence and Respect

Discuss reverence and respect as a feature of spirituality. (pp. 555–556)

Contemplative Practices

How does the contemplative stance form a part of spirituality? (p. 557)

POSSIBLE PAPER TOPICS

1. Research and discuss accommodations to the modern world achieved in a religious group of your choice.

2. Explore the principle of separation of church and state and how it is being applied in the United States today.

3. A lot of recent scholarship and discussion has occurred on the relationship between science and religion in the modern world. Review the findings and take a position.

INTERRELIGIOUS COMPARISONS

1. Investigate other features of fundamentalism, and then compare and contrast fundamentalist movements in two religions of your choice.

2. Explore the successes and challenges of those engaged in interfaith dialogue. What is the overall purpose and what are the ground rules for such encounters?

3. Explore how the traditional religions of Christianity and Islam are rethinking the place of nature in their religious understanding.

REFLECTION EXERCISES

1. This reflection is actually a bit of a challenge. The author of the text has given ample illustrations from music, photography, painting, and other areas that demonstrate the three aspects of eclectic spirituality—interrelatedness, reverence and respect, and the contemplative stance. Develop a multimedia presentation on one of the three features that somehow conveys an experience of that aspect.

2. Review the changes and challenges religion faces in the modern world, then review the practices and beliefs of a religion of your choice. Now imagine you have gone through some kind of a space-time rift and returned five hundred or a thousand years from now. How is the religion, if it still exists, being practiced and conceived?

3. Many of the role models for the Naturism movement are women. Notice that three of the four listed in the text have directly centered their work around animals. As traditional religions rethink the role of nature in their religious understandings, they also must consider animals. Already in 1993 an international group of Catholic and Protestant biblical scholars concluded that animals have just as much a possibility of getting into heaven as human beings. Imagine ways this new thinking about animals could influence religious beliefs and practices.

4. In the text, the author demonstrated how secular philosophies like Communism or events like a rock concert manifest features of religion. Explore other areas like the courtroom or a football game to identify religious features and practices that appear.

5. After studying many of the world's major religions and investigating the religious search in the modern world, you are now in a position to possibly define a religious experience. They occur in religious settings and in nature. And the author says that they sometimes occur in nontraditional places, like watching a movie or experiencing music. What have been the spiritual experiences of you and your friends and where have they occurred?

ANSWERS

Fill In the Blank

1. globalism
2. multiculturalism
3. modern capitalism
4. parochialism
5. secularism
6. agnosticism
7. environmentalism
8. fundamentalism
9. ecotourism
10. naturism

Multiple Choice

1. c
2. d
3. a
4. d
5. c
6. b
7. a
8. d
9. c
10. b
11. a
12. d
13. c

APPENDIX

INTERNET RESOURCES FOR WORLD ART

Asian Art Museum of San Francisco
http://www.asianart.org

Centre Georges Pompidou
http://www.cnac-gp.fr/

Fine Arts Museum of San Francisco
http://www.thinker.org

Florence Art Guide
http://www.mega.it/eng/egui/hogui.htm

Giverny (Monet's gardens)
http://www.giverny.org/index.htm

Guggenheim Museum in Bilbao
http://www.bm30.es/guggenheim

Hellenic Ministry of Culture
http://www.culture.gr

Kyoto National Museum
http://www.kyohaku.go.jp

The Louvre
http://www.louvre.fr

Museum of Modern Art
http://www.moma.org

The Smithsonian
http://www.si.edu

Uffizi Gallery
http://www.uffizi.firenze.it/welcomeE.html

Vatican Museum
http://www.christusrex.org/www1/vaticano/0-Musei.html

World Wide Web Virtual Library: Museums
http://www.comlab.ox.ac.uk/archive/other/museums.html.